The Outdoor Shower

The Outdoor Shower

Creative Design Ideas for Backyard Living, from the Functional to the Fantastic

Ethan Fierro

Storey Publishing

*The mission of Storey Publishing is to serve our customers by
publishing practical information that encourages
personal independence in harmony with the environment.*

Edited by Deborah Balmuth and Carleen Madigan Perkins
Art direction by Kent Lew and Vicky Vaughn
Cover design by Karen Schober and Kent Lew
Text design by Karen Schober
Text production by Kristy MacWilliams
Cover and interior photographs © Ethan Fierro
Illustrations © Robert LaPointe
Indexed by Christine R. Lindemer, Boston Road Communications

Printed in China by R.R. Donnelley
10 9 8 7 6 5 4 3 2

LIBRARY OF CONGRESS CATALOGING-IN-PUBLICATION DATA

Fierro, Ethan.
 The outdoor shower / by Ethan Fierro.
    p. cm.
 Includes index.
  ISBN 978-1-58017-552-4 (pbk. : alk. paper)
  ISBN 978-1-58017-606-4 (hardcover : alk. paper)
  1. Showers (Plumbing fixtures) I. Title: Outdoor shower. II. Title.
TH6492.F54 2006
696'.182—dc22   2005034731

Cool summer evening
illumined fireflies become
lighthouses in steam

**To the beloved Moosi and all who appreciate
deeply residing in hot water.**

Contents

Introduction

· · · · · · · · · · · · · ·

SHOWERING OUTDOORS is one of the greatest ways to connect with the wonder and beauty of the natural world. Standing outside, washing away the stresses of a long day, while enjoying your natural surroundings creates peace of mind and a new level of relaxation. This delightful moment may be one that you'll look forward to repeating every day, year after year.

In addition to their practical nature — washing off sand and dirt outside helps keep the interior of your house clean — showering outdoors also creates a sense of freedom that comes with bathing in a place set away from the pace of daily life. Add to that feeling a degree of personal satisfaction from having created this sanctuary yourself, utilizing your favorite materials, and you have the makings of a memorable showering experience.

I grew up in the woods of Martha's Vineyard using an outdoor shower my father built. It was a semicircular enclosure he had created by driving posts into the ground in a large curve and bending soaked cedar boards around the face. Over time, English ivy grew up the wall and over the open latticework on top, giving a lush appearance to the enclosure.

I loved using that shower. The open sky above, where the steam rose and dissipated, and the finely carved wooden door latch that made a soft yet distinct "shah-thunk" sound every time the door closed: all are beloved memories that have stayed with me through the years. That outdoor shower opened my eyes to a new way of working with my environment, and my father's artistic example has inspired me in my own architectural designs.

I hope that, in addition to giving you a basic understanding of how outdoor showers work, the different options for materials and construction, and how to go about creating your own design, this book will also inspire you to think differently about the environment around you. Your outdoor shower project is waiting to begin.

ABOVE: The last drops of water fall from a curved showerhead pipe simply affixed to a wooden board pedestal.

OPPOSITE: This oceanfront shower on Martha's Vineyard, Massachusetts, is constructed of weathered white cedar stakes attached to a curved metal frame.

CHAPTER 1

Shower Basics

· · · · · · · · · · · · ·

ESSENTIALLY, THE OUTDOOR SHOWER, like its indoor counterpart, is a simple plumbing system with common components — water supply, water drainage, plumbing, and fixtures. Most people like to shower with hot water, so water heating should also be considered. And because of its location outdoors, proper siting, enclosures, and lighting are additional variables that will affect how enjoyable your outdoor shower is to actually use.

There are other practical elements to consider while you are designing your shower that will help you determine what kind of structure to build and where to locate it. Will it be in operation seasonally or year-round? If seasonally, is it in a region that freezes in the winter? If it is, the plumbing will require drainage valves to be installed, and you'll need to drain the pipes before winter to

keep them from bursting. How much privacy should the shower offer? Some people prefer to have a complete visual barrier between themselves and potential onlookers, while others would rather not block the view of the surrounding landscape. It's often prudent to build for the most modest personality in the crowd, to allow everyone to enjoy the outdoor showering experience.

Material quality is a key factor in the longevity of your shower. The more durable the building materials are, the longer the lifespan your shower will have. For example, using cement, metal, or wooden products that thrive in all climatic conditions will allow for decades of enjoyment. The aesthetic qualities of the materials you choose also should not be overlooked; you'll want your shower to be attractive as well as durable. In the end, the quality of the showering experience will be enhanced by the quality of the materials used in building the shower — and you should aim for the best showering experience your budget will allow.

Finding the Right Spot

Choosing the location for your outdoor shower is a decision that will have far-reaching impact on all the other stages of design, construction, and use. Your outdoor shower's placement in the environment will affect the amount of privacy you'll have when you're using it, how your shower accentuates the surrounding architecture and landscaping (and, conversely, how the surrounding architecture and landscaping affect your showering experience), what degree of technology is required to operate the mechanical systems, and the materials that will be most desirable for meeting the needs of all of your shower's functional and aesthetic considerations.

When choosing the location for your shower (shower styles are covered in detail in chapter 3) you need to predetermine what kind of shower you want to build in order to then find a location that will be suitable for your design. When building a permanent shower around your home, great care will be required to make sure that the location is suitable for your needs, as you will live with this choice well into the future. However, if you want to erect a temporary shower in your yard just for a season, then by all means, try one location the first season, and another the next year.

OPPOSITE: The shoulder-high Douglas fir enclosure of this shower gives bathers some privacy, while still affording them a view of the ocean in the distance.

Here are a few points to consider in your quest to identify the ideal outdoor shower site:

- Do you want the shower in an out-of-the-way location, offering privacy not only by design but also from remoteness?

- Is accessibility an important factor? If so, consider locating the shower next to an exterior door or often-used pathway for the sake of convenience.

- Do you want to make use of any pre-existing structural support such as exterior walls, decks, overhanging eaves, trellises, stairways, paths, or alcoves? If so, then envision how you can seamlessly incorporate your shower into these areas. Taking advantage of existing structures is a way to conserve materials and make the most of what you already have.

- An old adage for the homeowner when siting a house is to locate it in the most unappealing space on the land so that you end up viewing the beautiful areas from this location. The same could hold true for the location of your shower — place it in a spot that is relatively unappealing to look at, but which has an attractive view.

- Gather all of the people (family, presumably) who will be living with and using the shower. Have everyone go outside and separately walk around and write down his or her top three locations of choice. Then reconvene and discuss why they made the choices they did. Focus on the overlap of areas (if there were any), and begin to narrow your search through a consensual decision-making process.

You must also consider the challenges your potential shower site will offer for construction. You'll need to assess the best way to access the area for importing building materials. Is there adequate room for a truck to deliver materials to the site? If not, where will those materials be delivered, and how will you get them to the site? Will you or your contractor have room to navigate the site with tools and machinery? If space is tight or access awkward, you may need to brainstorm ways to make movement around the site easier and safer.

Water Supply

Water is the element that makes the shower a shower; without it you are high and dry. Depending on the geographical region where you're building your shower, water can be accessed from many different sources, including private wells, municipal water supplies, rain catchments (especially in arid regions with dwindling water supplies, or in certain tropical environments where there is bountiful rain and a poor water table), ponds or lakes, rivers, thermal hot springs, and even desalinization plants (such as in ocean-bordering desert regions). The trick is in getting that water to your shower.

If your outdoor shower is going to be located near your home, the best source of water for it is your home's plumbing system. The plumbing can simply be extended to the exterior of the building at the location where it passes closest to your shower's intended location. In colder regions, however, the exterior extension of the plumbing will need to be winterized (see page 21).

A Vermont stream is funneled through ancient water-worn stone, creating the perfect natural outdoor shower. If you're lucky enough to live in such a setting, the stream may also provide water for your constructed outdoor shower.

Outdoor showers are most often connected to the household plumbing system. In this scenario, water enters the system in the basement, from a well pump or municipal supply line. The line then splits in two: one line feeds into a hot water heater (and then supplies the house and outdoor shower with hot water) and the other line delivers cold water.

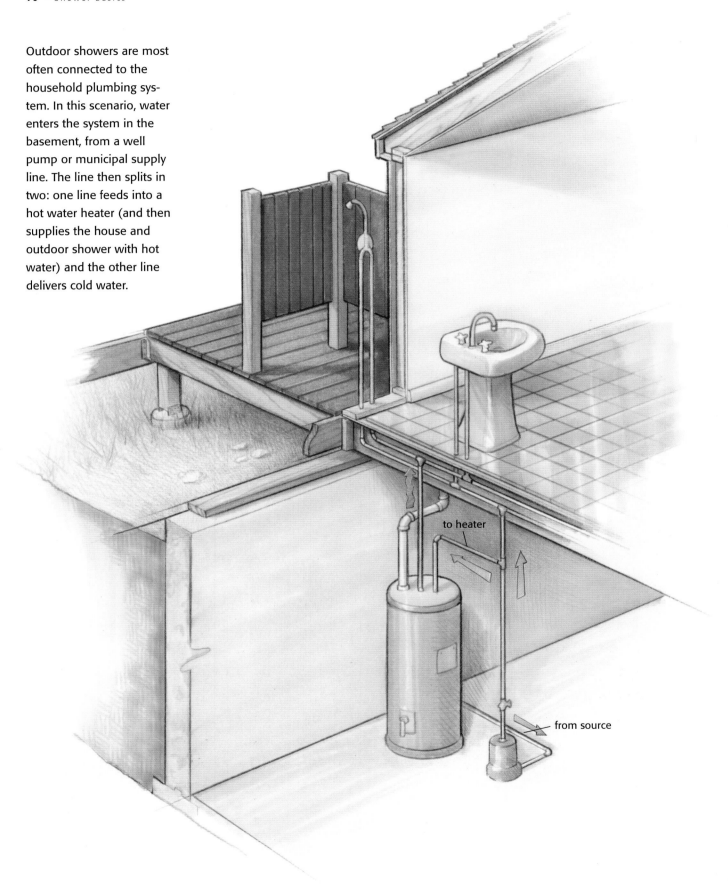

to heater

from source

Cisterns

A rooftop storage tank or cistern can also be used to supply water to an outdoor shower. Often the cistern system is a necessity of the location; it may be the only option for acquiring fresh water in a dry environment where a deep well would otherwise be required. Some households in tropical locales store rooftop rain catchment water, which is plentiful, in cisterns. Rooftop cisterns are also used on islands where the water table is unreliable or is infiltrated by seawater, making groundwater nonpotable. High-rise urban housing environments also utilize rooftop cistern technology, as the gravitational force of a cistern-operated system provides plenty of natural pressure for the building's plumbing system. (This water, however, is not from rain catchment but is pumped up to the roof from a distant reservoir.)

Cisterns typically hold a very large volume of water, anywhere from 1,000 to 25,000 gallons (3.8 to 94.6 kL). Considering the physical forces at work when large volumes of water are being collected in a container, cisterns are complex to engineer and construct. The builder should be well versed with all structural and engineering requirements for the site location, intended volume of storage, and construction materials.

Hot Water

Though you must have water to have a shower, you don't necessarily need *hot* water. A case in point is the camp shower, where you may be washing "on the run," and don't really care if the water is hot or not. Or if there is no sun to heat a portable solar shower (see page 104) and you don't want to heat water on a stove and mix up a comfortable bath for yourself, then you will have to settle for the ambient-temperature water on hand. Similarly, in most tropical situations, the average ambient temperature is so mild that showering with only the unheated water on hand is fine.

However, if you want the option of a hot shower, then there must be a system in place for creating and delivering this heated water to your shower. There are a few different options for heating the water using various kinds of energy and technology.

Household Tank Heaters

As the main water supply line enters a building, the cold water line splits off, sending a main lead into a heater to exit as hot water, while the other line remains cold and will run parallel throughout the building with the hot line to provide the hot/cold option for all of the water-based appliances. The first type of water heater is the tank style. This is a cylindrical tank with an electric or fuel-burning element underneath that heats the water to a predetermined temperature. An anti-scald device is included, so that at no place in the building will the water come out so hot that it burns the unaware user. The water does have to start off hot enough, though, to remain hot when it is supplying the most distant faucet from the tank. A well-insulated hot-water pipe will have a minimal loss of heat over the course of the water's journey from tank to tap.

If you decide to hook up your outdoor shower to your household plumbing, it can become just one more of the fixtures that draw from the household hot and cold water lines.

WHILE YOU WERE GONE

Second-home owners take special note: When the plumbing in a house goes unused for months at a time, the water sitting in a tank hot-water heater will become "cooked" as it builds up high levels of hydrogen sulfide, leaving your house smelling of rotten eggs. To avoid this problem, turn off the hot-water heater if the building is going to be empty for an extended period. Also, if the building is going to be empty at a time when temperatures typically drop below freezing, then the entire plumbing system should be drained and the toilets filled with antifreeze to prevent pipes from bursting.

On-Demand Heaters

Since the traditional tank-style water heater consumes copious amounts of fuel (because it maintains a volume of water at a high temperature continuously), some energy-conscious home owners are choosing to install on-demand water heaters. An on-demand heater flash-heats the water you need only when the hot water faucet is opened. The rest of the time, the water is held at room temperature. This is an efficient approach to water heating because extra energy is not needlessly consumed for hot water storage. In addition, the on-demand heaters are small compared to traditional water heaters and thus require less storage space. They also tend to require less maintenance and cost less to operate. On-demand heaters may also be preferable for second-home owners (see "While You Were Gone," this page).

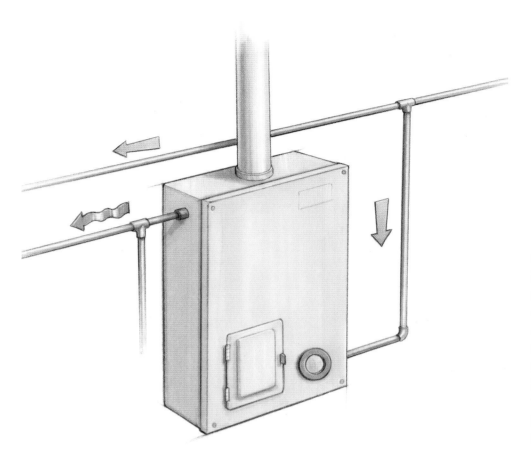

On-demand heaters flash-heat water only when needed, saving on energy costs. The cold line bifurcates before entering the unit, sending water through the heater for as long as the shower is on. The heater immediately shuts downs when the shower is turned off.

Solar Heaters

A low-impact option for heating water to supply your outdoor shower is a solar-powered system. The solar system works by harnessing energy from the sun and converting it to heat and electricity. Solar collectors in the form of photovoltaic panels convert the sun's energy into electricity that can power a water circulation pump. This pump moves cold water through a solar heater, which collects energy from the sun to significantly raise the water's temperature. Once heated, the hot water is pumped into a storage tank, where it can later be accessed and mixed with cold water as necessary in the shower. If you are building a solar-heated outdoor shower, then you need to run only a cold-water supply line out to the shower location. At the shower location, the supply line should split, with one line entering the solar heating coils and the other feeding cold water directly into the shower.

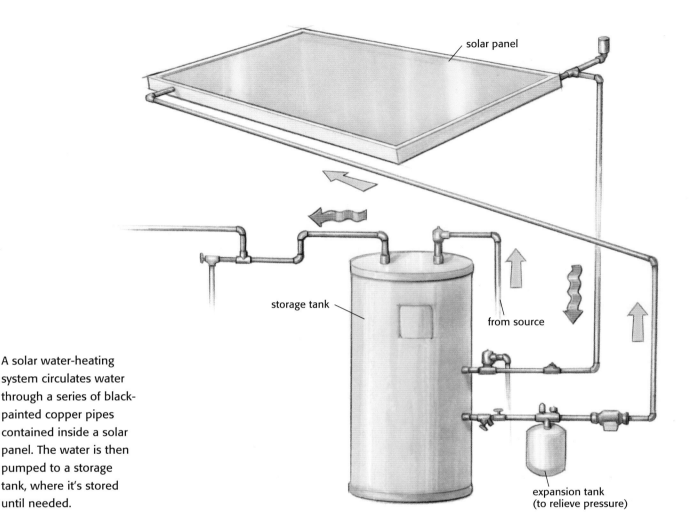

solar panel

storage tank

from source

expansion tank
(to relieve pressure)

A solar water-heating system circulates water through a series of black-painted copper pipes contained inside a solar panel. The water is then pumped to a storage tank, where it's stored until needed.

This kind of solar system is an "active" system, using mechanical components to warm the water. A "passive" system simply absorbs the heat of the sun, with no mechanics involved; the solar shower described in chapter 4, which employs a black plastic bag to absorb heat from the sun, is a passive solar system. Both types of solar heating make use of a free and unlimited resource. Solar technology is viable for those people who live off the power grid and have consistent sunlight to work with; it also can be used to supplement a fuel-burning system, for example by using the energy of the sun to do the initial work of turning cold water into warm water, and using a propane or electric unit to make the warmed water hot enough for use. This method, in which solar and petroleum- or electricity-based technologies work in conjunction with each other, is a "middle-of-the-road" compromise that makes use of the best of both worlds.

Plumbing Considerations

The household plumbing system is a series of interconnected pipes, valves, faucets, heaters, pumps, and reservoir tanks that deliver both hot and cold water to the various outlets in a home or secondary buildings operating off the same plumbing system. When installing an outdoor shower, an additional section of plumbing will have to be added to the pre-existing system in order to supply water for exterior usage. In order to accomplish this, a section of the main household plumbing system will have to be shut down, depressurized, and drained so that the plumber can have empty plumbing to work with when splicing in the new pipes. Once the shower is installed, the zone is repressurized and turned back on.

This task is potentially within the capabilities of a well-informed person armed with a small collection of specialized tools. However, depending on the complexity of the plumbing system of the main structure, you'll want to carefully assess the situation to judge whether you feel capable of taking on this stage of the construction process. You'll also want to check with your local building codes and make sure a licensed plumber inspects your work.

SHUTTING DOWN FOR THE WINTER

If your outdoor shower is in a region that freezes during the winter, the plumbing will require a seasonal draining. If your shower is connected to a household plumbing system and the house will be vacant for the season, then the whole plumbing system (including the shower) should be drained. If the house will be in use during the winter, you'll need to install shut-off valves and drains in the feed lines that supply the shower.

To drain the pipes, begin by shutting off the water supply by closing the shut-off valves. In the shower, turn the shower control handles to the open position; most of the water will flow out. Go back to the supply pipes and find the screw caps of the drains, which are located on the bottom of the pipes on the shower side of the shut-off valves. Unscrew the caps; any remaining water in the pipes will be released. You might also blow out the pipes with an air compressor just to make sure that there isn't any trapped water that will rupture your plumbing.

When planning the plumbing for your outdoor shower, carefully consider how far hot water will have to travel from its source. Ideally, a shower should not be more than 100 to 125 feet (30 to 38 m) from the heating unit, so that the water will not have cooled off by the time it arrives at the showerhead. If a shower is going to be 125 feet (38 m) or more from the hot water supply, it should have its own hot water heater (such as the on-demand style described on page 18).

Plumbing Material Options

There are basically two pipe options to choose from for the plumbing of your outdoor shower: copper or chlorinated polyvinyl chloride (CPVC).

Copper. This is the industry standard for permanence, quality, and long-lasting reliable use. Rigid copper is the optimal material for water-supply pipes because of its smooth interior, which provides a friction-free water flow, and its inherent ability to resist corrosion. Equally durable with hot or cold temperatures, rigid copper tubing is typically used in ½-inch (12 mm) and ¾-inch (19 mm) dimensions. One-inch (25 mm) copper pipe is available for larger feed lines in situations where the shower is far away from the water storage source. Copper fittings are used to connect lengths of straight pipe and create angled turns. All joints are soldered, creating a strong bond that will provide decades of trouble-free operation.

CPVC. This plastic product is less expensive than copper and is not the first choice for custom-designed and custom-built outdoor showers. Rather, CPVC is best used for temporary, portable, or transient shower applications, such as for camping, festivals, hunting, low-impact eco-tourism, and so on. You get the picture. CPVC is cheap, lightweight, and easy to connect and detach. It won't cost a lot to outfit your camp with an easy-to-build shower using CPVC.

Be sure to have on hand extra pipes, fittings, primer, and some epoxy when assembling a CPVC-plumbed shower on location, as adjustments and repairs may be required. Compared to copper, this material can be damaged easily. Sometimes, a quick fix is all that's needed to keep the shower in operation.

OPPOSITE: This simple pedestal shower is constructed from 3-inch galvanized pipe. Brackets support two ½-inch copper showerheads that have been fashioned from simple end-cap fittings. All of these materials are easily found at most hardware or plumbing-supply stores.

ALWAYS THE RIGHT TEMPERATURE

• • • • • • • •

In tropical environments, some showers offer only one water temperature — ambient. The pleasure of using an ambient-temperature shower can vary depending on your comfort level throughout the day (or night), but water supplied in these situations is generally in the realm of 60 to 75°F (16 to 24°C).

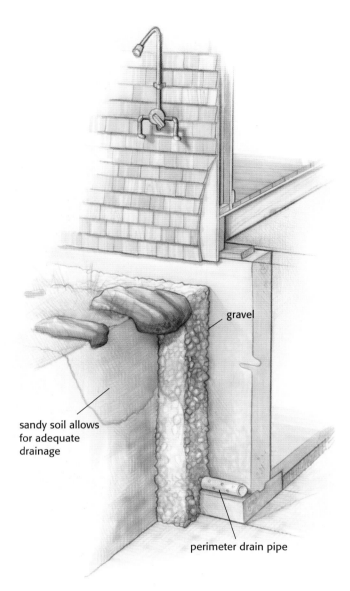

gravel

sandy soil allows
for adequate
drainage

perimeter drain pipe

In sites where the soil is
sandy and has a high per-
colation rate, no additional
construction may be
needed for water drainage.

Water Drainage

Shower wastewater, known as graywater, needs to be channeled to a safe place where it will become contained, purified, and eventually returned to its active role in maintaining a healthy water table. Depending on your local building codes and the frequency with which your shower will be used, you may be able to create a simple graywater percolation system. If you're building an outdoor shower in the city or another area where there's little or no soil to filter the graywater, it's likely you'll want the shower to drain into a municipal sewage system. The basic options are as follows.

Let It Fall

Drainage can be as simple as allowing the graywater to fall onto the ground, where it will become absorbed and filtered back into the earth. This is a common approach often employed where the soil is very sandy or percolates well; so long as the water has nowhere to build up and collect (causing stagnation issues and creating an environment in which insects will breed), it is generally safe. However, you should check on local building codes to make sure that your shower drainage complies with them, as this surface runoff option is not legal in some areas.

Dig a Dry Well

If you want to drain the graywater from your shower into the ground but the soil is not sandy enough to absorb the water directly, you will have to install a dry well. This is simply a layer of gravel beneath the shower that allows the graywater to percolate down into the earth, where it eventually seeps into the soil, becoming purified as it filters through the layers of dirt, sand, and stone. The water has no chance to pool or build up, thus creating a cleaner, safer, and more appealing environment in which to bathe.

You'll want to dig the dry well before you begin construction of the shower enclosure. Begin by marking out the intended perimeter of the shower. Add an extra 16 inches (41 cm) all around; this new perimeter marks the edges of the hole you will dig. Find a convenient location to dump all the soil that will come out of this hole — there will be a lot of it. Then start digging, down to a depth of 3 to 4 feet (0.9 to 1.2 m). Once the hole is dug, fill it with ¾-inch (19 mm) crushed gravel.

heavy soil

gravel dry well

A dry well — essentially an excavated area filled with gravel — is a simple way to deal with wastewater in sites that have heavy soil.

RINSE FEET BEFORE SHOWERING

• •

If your outdoor shower is in a beach or lakeside area and you have connected the shower drain to your septic or municipal line, let me offer a word of caution. Keep a tray of fresh water by the entrance to the shower and ask bathers to rinse their feet in it before entering the shower. This will prevent excess sand from being tracked in and rinsed down the drain, potentially clogging up the septic tank or plumbing.

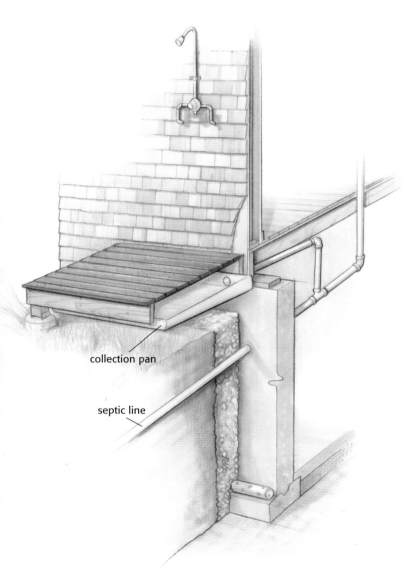

collection pan

septic line

A shower pan installed under the bathing platform collects wastewater and channels it into the house-hold septic system. Alternatively, water collected in the pan can be redirected and used to irrigate land-scape plantings.

Install a Shower Pan

A third option is to install a shower pan underneath the shower stall area. As is the case for an indoor shower, a plastic, fiberglass, metal, or rubber-lined shower pan beneath an outdoor shower contains the graywater and directs it to a drain. The pan could connect to the system that manages the rest of your household wastewater, whether that is a municipal line or a private septic tank with an attached leach field.

The water from a shower pan can also be used to irrigate ornamental gardens (however, it is not safe to drain unfiltered graywater from the shower into areas near food-producing plants). Simply run a length of flexible 2-inch (5 cm) hose from the drain in the pan, and use that water to irrigate trees, shrubs, and flower gardens.

The Shower Floor

The most important characteristics of the shower floor are that it be nonslippery and able to direct the used water to the drainage system, whether that is a sand-based soil surrounding the shower, the dry well, or a direct connection with the household wastewater system.

If the shower is installed on a deck, you may choose to use the decking itself for the floor of the shower (as long as it's made from non-splintering wood). For this arrangement to work, the deck must be suspended above the ground, with space below for air to circulate and dry the decking boards after the shower has been used. Also, the decking boards must have at least a ¼-inch space between them to allow the water to fall through to the drainage system below.

If you want the shower on ground level, you could pour a concrete slab with a center drain that evacuates the graywater. You may want to set stones with a slightly rough surface into the concrete slab to create a comfortable and safe surface to stand on. Another option is to install a dry well and seat stones on top of the well's gravel to ensure comfortable footing for bathers.

Yet another option for a shower floor is a combination of a dry well for drainage and an elevated wooden platform for comfortable footing. After digging the dry well and filling it with gravel (as described on page 25), you'll also need to make sure the gravel is compacted with a jumping jack or other gas-powered compacting device. Compacting prevents future settling of the gravel, which is important because the gravel will not only be evacuating water from the shower, it will also serve as the base for concrete footings and foundation posts to support the platform. This design is very resilient in cold climates, as it prevents moisture from becoming trapped below the footings and heaving them out of the ground during freezing weather.

Cedar decking provides for comfortable footing in this outdoor shower cabana. Graywater from the shower is collected in a pan under the deck.

Walls and Enclosures

In order to decide on the type of enclosure (or lack thereof) your shower will have, you'll want to review the vast range of options. Partitioning can be created out of literally anything. You can have an impenetrable screen around the shower — such as a solid wooden wall — so that no light passes through. Slats, either horizontal or vertical, can be affixed to a structural framework with an overlapping design to ensure complete privacy. Such slats could also be affixed at spaced intervals so that a calibrated amount of light and air can pass through. Another solid partitioning material commonly employed in outdoor showers is stone, whether as fieldstones in a wall or as large, flat slabs creating a visual barrier. Again, spaces can be left between the stones to allow light and air to pass through.

Other materials that perform in a similar fashion to create a solid or semisolid enclosure include bamboo poles or culms, rattan or similar grasslike stalks, glass blocks, wire mesh with stucco applied to the surface, corrugated metal panels, thick grapevines woven together, and beaded curtains. Think of this list as a beginning, not an end. There are as many materials available for use as there are open minds discovering their uses, so keep your eyes open.

Vegetative screening is largely semisolid, allowing for the free flow of light and air in and out of your shower while retaining a nominal degree of privacy. A simple form of vegetative screening is a wire mesh frame that has flowering vines growing over it. Of course, in climates where vegetation dies back on a seasonal basis, such a screen is more visually open at certain times of the year. Along these same aesthetic lines, metal poles could be installed in a relatively tight configuration, with 2 to 4 inches (3 to 5 cm) between them, in a foundation of concrete. They alone could act as a semisolid screening device, or some kind of vegetative matter could be planted at the base, allowing for all of these strong, vertical lines to become softened. Ornamental grasses can be planted side by side to form an enclosure around the shower, creating a wonderfully soft and bushy environment in which to bathe. Many grasses thrive on the moisture and some will grow long stalks with puffy plumes at the top that look gorgeous during the cold season. A screen of fast-growing white pine trees or bamboo is also a prime choice for providing a delightful showering enclosure. These suggestions may or may not work for your particular region, but most likely you will be able to find comparable plantings for your area.

This rental cabin at
The Apple Farm in Philo,
California, makes creative
use of corrugated galva-
nized metal panels. The
spiraled ½-inch copper
pipe lends an artistic flourish to the strong horizontal
and vertical lines.

Lastly, you can choose to have no enclosure at all. This type of shower offers the wide-open feeling of purely being in nature on nature's terms . . . no separation. It is a wonderful feeling to bathe and cleanse uninhibitedly, by yourself or with like-minded friends or family. Though not for everyone, this approach finds its home where people are comfortable being physically exposed and sharing in the beauty of the natural world.

Fixtures

Temperature-control handles and showerheads come in a dizzying array of shapes, sizes, styles, and finishes. You may find yourself drawn to modern styles, reproduction fittings that aesthetically hearken back to days of old, or perhaps reconditioned antiques that bear the authentic look of time and age. Another option is to retrofit an object that is designed for some other purpose but works perfectly well as a fitting for your outdoor shower; standard garden-faucet lever controls, for example, work well as temperature-control handles. Explore your options, and discover the unexpected possibilities that present themselves.

The scope of accessories that are contained in the category of "fittings" also include floor grills, drain covers, mirrors, soap dishes, towel racks, shelving, clothing hooks, and any other accoutrement that makes your shower more user-friendly. These elements are both functional and decorative, setting the tone for your personal aesthetic. Always keep an eye out for ways to accessorize your shower. The simplest details can make a big difference.

Door handles and latches are always an opportunity to reveal hidden elements of delight, whether they are purchased from a street-side vendor in Nepal, or nature-aged pieces of wood found in the forest or on the beach. It doesn't take much to usher forth a sense of gaiety and fun that everyone using the shower will appreciate.

Showerhead Height

The height of the shower should allow for comfortable headroom. The plumbing industry standard is to install the showerhead at a height of 6½ feet (1.98 m). This height allows bathers of almost any height to use the shower comfortably. However, if very tall bathers will routinely use the shower, you may want to set the showerhead even higher.

OPPOSITE: The creative, vining copper plumbing and sheet-metal foliage of this shower on Cumberland Island, Georgia, add an aesthetic touch to the most functional part of the shower.

Showerheads

The hinged plumbing of this broad, polished-chrome showerhead gives the option for customized positioning of the water flow.

This hand-carved wooden fixture in the form of Peter Pan channels water for an impromptu shower when it rains.

Twin showerheads, attached to weathered cedar boards, offer side-by-side showering for friends.

A specially designed sunflower showerhead lends a sense of playfulness to this Tucson, Arizona, shower.

Handles and Hooks

• • • • • • • • • • •

This decorative dragon handle was purchased from a streetside vendor in Nepal.

A handmade wooden handle has been attached to the diagonal support of this door, rather than at the edge of it.

Using natural materials, like this towel hook made from a mountain laurel branch, adds an organic flair to outdoor showers.

A cast-bronze dragonfly clothes hook adorns a mottled pine board.

Lighting the Shower

Lighting can play a key role, both aesthetically and functionally, in your outdoor shower. Night is one of the most wonderful times to enjoy the pleasures of bathing outside. With proper lighting, your shower can take on an entirely new personality. Depending on the type of lighting unit you choose, where you place it, and how you direct its light, this added element can greatly accentuate the beauty of your shower.

- Nautical-grade deck lights can be installed in the floor of your shower, illuminating the entire room from ground level. These units are designed to withstand the rigorous conditions of the yachting environment and are the optimal choice for lights in the "wet zone."

- Down-wash lamps provide a mellow, warm glow from beneath the lamp housing, offering a soft ambient light and a generally soothing atmosphere that is perfect for walls and pathways.

- Floodlights are used to direct a wide beam of light over an area to illuminate walls, trees, and other special features of the structure or landscape.

- Spotlights project a focused beam of light, pinpointing a single dominant point of visual interest.

Note that lights that will be mounted outdoors have to be of exterior-grade quality, offering a waterproof gasket to weather the normal degree of moisture associated with being in the rain.

Controlling your lighting system through a rheostat dimmer switch will give you the option of adjusting the amount of light emitted from your lighting system at any given time. After investing so much time and energy in the construction of your outdoor shower, why limit the possibilities of ambience? With a simple dimmer switch, you can fine-tune the degree of atmosphere so that it perfectly suits the tenor of any particular evening. Choreographing the ambience to the mood of your guests as they enjoy an evening bath is a special treat they won't soon forget.

Specialty lighting design companies offer computer-controlled systems that can be preprogrammed for modes for illumination. You can set them to create different lighting scenarios to match the time of evening or night, weather conditions, and areas of your yard that may benefit from special highlighting at various times of the season. This degree of technical sophistication would require the expertise of an electrician and potentially a design consultant. However, even with just a cache of low-voltage lighting fixtures and an electrical timer, you can create a stunning environment for nighttime shower enjoyment.

Lighting the Shower Path

Along with lighting in the shower, lighting along the walkway will benefit the nighttime bather greatly. The walkway lighting, like the shower itself, can be understated or overt in its appearance. Lighting features can stand out alone as individual illuminated guide posts or they can recede unobtrusively into the landscape along the side of the path.

A set of low-key down-wash lights following the course of the path is perfect for this purpose. The lights can be wired to an electrical system that is controlled from within the main building, or they can be individually powered by a little solar panel in the top of each lamp's housing. There are many types of these products on the market; see the appendix on page 138.

A copper lantern illuminates the walkway near a step. A series of these look gorgeous lining a path during the day and provide for safe passage after the sun goes down.

Another option for lighting the path is fixed or hanging copper lamps. These durable, weather-resilient products are relatively inexpensive. They are powered by an electrical line that is controlled from the main building, and their brightness can be adjusted with a rheostat dimmer. Like copper plumbing, copper lamps weather to a low luster and develop a patina of verdigris. Delicately placed among various plants and shrubs lining your walkway, these lamps are a shoo-in for understated utilitarian beauty. Place them close enough together that the circles of light cast down on the ground intersect with each other, leaving no footfall in the dark.

There are, of course, inexpensive plastic versions of these copper lamps that provide a similar service. Inevitably they cost less but are not as durable, being subject to ultraviolet degradation. Just remember that you get what you pay for.

OPPOSITE: This stone lantern, illuminated with fiber-optic cable, lights the way to a fully detached shower.

THE BALANCED LANTERN

• • • • • • • • • • • • • • • • •

In my own work, I have developed balanced stone lanterns to light clients' pathways. These lanterns are a combination of various elements, and each is unique. First is the beauty found in the natural shape of the stone itself; two or three stones balanced and pinned together create a striking sculptural expression. This stack can range in height from 2 to 8 feet (0.6 to 2.4 m). In the right setting, these large or small lanterns can accentuate various focal points of the terrain.

The featured aspect of these lanterns is the balanced shape of the form. When a gravity-defying posture is attained, "stone liberation" occurs. The eyes see that the stones are standing, yet the mind thinks, "These things should fall over." This is the moment when magic happens.

We are accustomed to seeing stone below us or resting in a stationary position, so when we are presented with stones (sometimes very large ones) standing upright in the air, they take on strong personalities.

The light is provided by a rectangular socket or mortise in the lantern that receives a light feature. This could be a fluorescent, incandescent, fiber-optic, or LED (light-emitting diode) light or simply a candle set behind a pane of frosted glass framed with copper or bronze. The combination of a statue of stones with a glowing light panel creates an amazing silhouette against a darkening sky. The effect of seeing a line of these balanced lanterns leading you meanderingly down the garden path is extraordinary.

The Kahua Hawaiian Institute

Maui, Hawaii

THIS HAWAIIAN RETREAT CENTER IS HOST to several extraordinary outdoor showers. The first is a semi-detached glass-block enclosure built into the deck of a guest cottage overlooking the Pacific Ocean, simultaneously offering a superb shower and an extraordinary focal element. Glass block offers a stable and efficient way to frame in and create an "illuminated" showering stall, whether using natural light during the day or glowing with nautical-grade lamps at night.

Another semi-detached Kahua Hawaiian Institute creation is the mermaid shower, which is truly a unique variation on the theme. Complete with a dolphin foot-cleaning spigot, the shower offers bathers all they need for an entertaining showering experience. Basalt makes up the structural body of the rear wall, while stucco and tile finish off the interior face.

A third Kahua Hawaiian Institute shower is a mix of Southwestern-style stucco construction and Hawaiian iconography. Mixed together, they produce a wonderful enclosure in which bathers feel the organic curvature of a structure that seems to have risen out of the land itself. The carefully chosen statues and devotional objects placed in alcoves and recesses lend a sense of peace and quietude.

LEFT: A freeform stucco shower features alcoves for devotional objects.

OPPOSITE: This glass-block enclosure illuminates a bather on the deck of a guest cottage.

CHAPTER 2

Choosing Building Materials

· · · · · · · · · · · · ·

AS IS THE CASE WITH ALL CREATIVE PROJECTS, the best outdoor showers result when design and materials work in conjunction with one another. The quality of materials at your disposal is sometimes less important than what is created with them. If the design is strong and well grounded, and works in harmony with the location, then the beauty of the structure will follow suit. Good architecture follows design, not your ability to purchase expensive materials. Raw materials are all around us and can supply even the most ambitious of projects.

For example, a house, garage, and outdoor shower designed and built by a Southern California couple makes brilliant use of blocks of concrete sidewalks destroyed by earthquake. A huge pile of rubble blocks was trucked to the house site, and with sledgehammers

the couple reduced the slabs into brick-size pieces. The vision was to build a 2,000-square-foot (186 sq m) house entirely with reclaimed/recycled materials. The concrete blocks became walls, reclaimed Douglas-fir bridge trestles became the massive post and beam framing, and the elegant outdoor shower (composed simply of a showerhead and control knobs) resides on a south-facing stucco wall.

Depending on what kinds of building materials you'll be using, there are many ways to locate and acquire supplies. There is always the mainstream approach of purchasing brand-name products at retail prices from home centers and lumberyards. Finding alternative methods for locating and acquiring

Stripped of their bark, these black locust timbers form a post-and-beam arbor for an outdoor shower.

materials can be beneficial to both your design and your budget. Reclaimed materials, if still sound of structure, can add quality and durability to your project while requiring only a fraction of the investment you might make in new materials. They also lend a sense of age and character. By visiting salvage yards, local stone quarries, and contractors' surplus stores, and by scouring your property for natural building supplies, you can bring to your shower project a broad scope of materials that will add a strong artistic flare.

Wood

Wood is among the most commonly used and versatile materials. Depending on their strength, durability, and appearance, some types of wood are best used in the structural framing of an outdoor shower; others can be used for handrails, floor grills, trellises, and door handles.

Wood is relatively easy to work with. You can cut, drill, screw, bolt, sand, polish, glue, and bend it. You can connect it to a host of other building materials. You can join together complementary species. And as long as all areas have free-flowing air around them and are able to dry out, wood will endure a fair amount of exposure while developing a beautiful patina with use.

There are many types of wood, each with its own distinct characteristics. For moist outside environments (such as in your outdoor shower), the type of wood that will act as your best ally will be from trees that have grown in or near water. When wet, these woods remain stable and retain their structural integrity, and they will not shift, shrink, or warp as they dry. The best examples of this kind of wood are black locust, cedar, and cypress. Mahogany, teak, and other types of extremely durable woods imported from places like Honduras, the Philippines, and various African and Southeast Asian countries would also fit the bill. But unless you are recycling or reusing them, their financial cost may be prohibitive, and the environmental toll of harvesting these woods on those regions can be catastrophic.

Black Locust

This tree grows wild and in profusion on the East Coast. It yields a tremendously stable wood historically renowned for its rot-resistant characteristics. Farmers used to sink untreated locust fence posts in the ground and claim that they would

"outlast their children's children." You might take that with a grain of salt, but I *have* seen 80-year-old locust posts that, despite a touch of rot right at ground level, were rock solid through and through.

Black locust wood ages beautifully when stripped of its bark. Peel a fresh black locust pole and within a year the weathering process will make it look like an old sun-bleached dinosaur bone. I've used black locust for the corner posts of teahouses, arbors, trellises, and massive bridge handrails. The grain is rather squirrelly, so unless you happen upon a rare pile of boards at a sawmill you will most likely find black locust wood by looking for the tree growing by the sides of roads or on the border of fields and asking the landowner if you can barter for some.

Western Red Cedar

Western red cedar grows in the Pacific Northwest and is a dark, reddish, soft wood used primarily for shingles (wall or roof), clapboards, interior or exterior paneling or trim, and large post and beam framing. It is on the softer end of the softwood spectrum, and as such, it dents and mars easily. It will last indefinitely outside (if it has free-flowing air around so it can dry out) and is pleasant to work with if your tools are very sharp. The sawdust has a sweetish scent, but I would caution against breathing it in; the particles are sharp and once lodged in your lungs won't readily come out.

This species is a fine choice for benches, slats on an arbor or trellis, shelving, trim boards on a door or around other types of openings, and a host of other locations where it won't suffer from frequent wear.

Western red cedar is used most often on the West Coast, as its availability is greater closer to the source. This is a fine choice if you can afford to use it.

Cypress

Various species of cypress grow in the United States in regions where water is plentiful. Cypress, like cedar, maintains its structural integrity for decades when installed in exterior conditions. Whether freshly milled or procured through salvage, cypress is at the top of the list for building enclosures, benches, decking, doors, and any number of other architectural details. It would be wasteful, however, unless you have access to vast quantities of cypress, to use it for any kind of hidden framing, as this beautiful wood should be used for decorative purposes as much as possible.

OPPOSITE: Weathered white cedar boards and frame highlight this shower attached to the exterior of a classic Cape Cod–style house. The small window is a whimsical touch, and allows the bather to enjoy the view while showering.

Douglas Fir

Douglas fir grows primarily in the Pacific Northwest. Its wood has a warm reddish hue and is very resinous, which gives it an inherent ability to withstand abuse from the elements. It's frequently used for decking, exterior trim, and unpainted finish work. This would be an optimal choice for the floor or grill of your outdoor shower. Douglas fir also makes fine handrails and, when sanded smooth and sealed with a wood preservative, will remain pleasant to the touch. This wood is relatively easy to find at most lumberyards, but contacting a specialty supplier will put you in touch with top-grade timbers.

CONSCIENTIOUS BUILDING

● ● ● ● ● ● ● ● ● ● ● ● ● ● ● ●

Conserving natural resources is important to me, so I always recommend using wood that is farmed, recycled, salvaged, reused, or in some way consciously managed as a resource. Your approach to a project is as important as the final product, and bringing your awareness to the source of your materials will add integrity to your creation, which in turn can give you a deeper feeling of satisfaction.

I once greatly enjoyed using salvaged redwood and cypress lumber that was harvested over a hundred years ago. Originally this wood was used to make massive beer, wine, and pickle barrels, and as I cut open these boards, the age-old essences were released and filled the air with rich aromas of fermentation. The boards were made from trees harvested from virgin forests, which was made apparent by the fact that they had 80 to 100 growth rings to the inch — the rings were packed so tight that I had to use a magnifying glass to count them. I was filled with awe as I used this wood, brought on by the knowledge of the ancientness of these trees. To realize that my entire life was but three-eighths of an inch of one of the boards I was cutting put something unspeakable into perspective.

Southern Yellow Pine

This tree grows in the forests of the South. Because it grows very quickly, it yields a low-grade wood when farmed, producing wide growth rings with huge variation in the sap deposits in the wood and leaving the finished boards with a quirky grain that is unstable and prone to warping. The pressure-treated wood that's widely sold utilizes farmed Southern yellow pine that undergoes a chemical impregnation process to make it very rot resistant. Although pressure-treated wood no longer contains arsenic, it still has a low level of toxicity and is best used in hidden structural framing that is away from human touch (and sight).

First-growth Southern yellow pine is a very resinous, dense wood with an extremely stable grain. It is possible to find salvaged Southern yellow pine flooring that is very old and still has a tremendous amount of life left in it. Any old

This shower enclosure is very simply constructed of wooden lattice and a colorful beaded curtain.

Southern yellow pine you can locate and clean up would be a fine addition to a shower project. Two pieces of advice, though: put some clear preservative on the wood when you are done, and be wary of splinters, because the grain is very sharp and fibrous.

Woods Not Recommended

Pine (white, red, or pitch), spruce, and hemlock all grow widely throughout the country in many different regions and climates. These woods are very soft and rot easily when used in exterior locations. People often use these woods for trim on the outside of homes, slathering on an ample amount of paint for protection and aesthetic appeal. This creates a two-fold potential problem: first is the maintenance issue of having to repaint every few years; the upkeep can be expensive. If the wood is not repainted, the paint will chip, peel, or get destroyed by ultraviolet degradation and the wood will rot. Second, even if the wood is repainted regularly, there still is the possibility of moisture being trapped under the paint, which also will cause the wood to rot. Quite frankly, I recommend that you steer away from using these woods for anything having to do with your shower.

TIPS FOR BUYING WOOD

When you're out shopping for wood, whether at a local lumberyard or a specialty wood supplier, allow yourself plenty of time to examine the material before purchasing anything. Begin by examining the end grain, which can give you some clues to the quality in the length of the board. Tight growth rings indicate a slower-growing tree, and thus a more stable grain. After inspecting the end of the board, pull out each piece and look it over carefully for straightness of grain, as well as for knots and other defects. Invest extra time up front to select the finest boards you can find. Your efforts will be rewarded by making all stages of the building process easier and more efficient, as well as leaving less room for error.

MATERIALS

Wood and Tile

Aged Douglas fir boards are off-set on either side of the framing to allow for better air circulation.

Green slate tiles and grout create a verdant background in an indoor-outdoor shower.

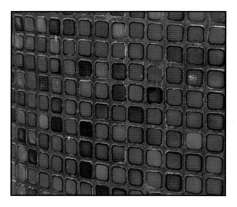

Blue-glazed ceramic tile creates a colorful and waterproof surface for warm-climate showers.

Mahogany boards spaced sideways make up this comfortable, well-aerated space for towelling off and dressing.

Stone and Brick

Multicolored slate forms a colorful patchwork walkway.

A combination of brick and stone create an interesting path to a remote outdoor shower.

Stone pavers can be laid for paths or used for building shower enclosures.

Lichen-covered granite and mortar form the foundation of an old outdoor shower.

Stone

Stone is an amazing material and comes in an extremely wide range of choices. Options range from the type of stone (that is, granite, slate, basalt, sandstone, marble, alabaster, and so on) to the various forms it comes in (naturally weathered, machine polished, in varying shapes, cut into dimensioned pieces, thermally treated with a stone torch to give a roughish nonslippery surface, and so on).

Bluestone

Bluestone, as its name implies, bears a bluish cast, and it is used extensively for patios, walkways, and pool decking because of its natural nonskid surface. It is a relatively soft stone that is easy to cut and shape with a few rudimentary tools, such as a diamond-bladed saw and stone chisels (hand or air powered). Bluestone is widely stocked by construction supply companies.

Slate

Relatively soft in composition, slate comes in various shades of gray, green, and black. This stone is smooth to the touch in a natural and unpolished condition, has an attractive matte or satin-like surface and is pleasurable to stand and sit on. The fine attributes that slate offers for outdoor shower construction can be put to use in wall paneling, walkway pads, bench and basin components, and decking to name but a few. Slate can be cut and shaped easily with a diamond-bladed saw, making it possible to contour around other stone, wood, or permanent design materials.

Marble

This classic stone creates an air of elegance wherever it is applied. Soft and malleable in nature, marble is found in black, white, green, or gray and variously streaked in color. Used for fountains, sculptures, basins, stairs, tiling, decking, fixtures, and accessories, this stone adds beauty and formality when incorporated into an outdoor shower environment.

Basalt

In the Hawaiian Islands and other volcanic environments, basalt, also known as lava stone, is the preferred choice of stone because of its plentitude. Being dark gray or black and very hard, it is elegant when used for walls, stairs, benches, and

OPPOSITE: The enclosure for this Tucson, Arizona, shower is a spiral of local fieldstone. Occasional slabs project out from the wall, creating shelves for sitting and holding bath products. A variety of sun-loving vines have been planted directly into the top of the wall.

pillars. When sliced into tile-thick wafers, basalt makes for an amazing floor or patio that sheds both water and sand. In your area, you may be able to find previously quarried pieces that were imported in the past century, when more quarries were actively mining basalt. There are companies that import basalt from other countries and can supply you with various shapes and sizes depending on your requirements.

Granite

Composing major areas of the bedrock in the United States, granite is a dense stone with a large proportion of quartz in its makeup. The fieldstones so often found in the old stone walls of New England are granite. This stone is quarried into blocks of any shape and size and is great for foundations, exposed finish work, and decorative applications. Anything from paths and steps to benches, structural supports, and planters could easily be made from this versatile stone.

Granite is often used as a building material, indoors and out. It can be found in in hundreds of different color variations, depending on where it's quarried.

Locating Stone

Quarries are common throughout the country, specializing in whatever type of stone is indigenous to their particular location. At most quarries you can order just about any configuration of stone imaginable to fit your needs. Another approach is to ask to see a quarry's "grout" pile. This is the place where hundreds of tons of excess stone scrap are dumped, and at a minimal cost you can procure some fantastic material. There are also salvage yards that specialize in stone products as well as stone supply houses, which sometimes operate in conjunction with a quarry and at other times independently. The selections and products available are nothing short of staggering.

If your design calls for stone, I suggest using resources that are close at hand and the most cost-effective. Collecting stones from the beach, combing salvage yards, sifting through grout piles at quarries, digging up rocks out of the ground, or calling landscaping contractors to find out whether you can buy from their personal stash — these approaches will ultimately save on material costs and lend a "natural" look to your outdoor shower environment.

Tile

There is an enormous selection of tile on the market in a wide array of materials ranging from ceramic to natural stone, porcelain, glass, cement, or metal. Because of its durability, tile can be used on the floor, walls, and ceiling of interior and exterior spaces. If you happen to live in an area that experiences below-freezing temperatures in winter, look for special tiles created to withstand the freeze/thaw conditions.

Tile can be rough or smooth, shiny or matte in luster, and overt or muted in color. It doesn't break down from ultraviolet degradation and can completely repel moisture. This material is so versatile that there is an appropriate style and quality for any environment, from kitchen and mudroom to shower stall.

Tile falls into two key groups: floor tile and wall (and ceiling) tile. Floor tile is relatively thicker than wall tile because it has to withstand the abusive conditions that floors are subject to. Floor tiles typically have a cast surface that keeps the floor from becoming slippery when wet. Though thicker, floor tile can be used on the walls of your shower if the surface or design is appealing. Let's explore the choices of tile you have to work with when designing your shower.

OPPOSITE: The mosaic of glazed ceramic tile in this Maui shower was created by the owner and depicts images inspired by the local undersea life.

PLACES TO FIND STONE

• • • • • • • • • • • • • • • •

■ **Local monument companies.** These businesses specialize in fabricating or finishing headstones. Ask about their willingness to detail stone for you, such as cutting, drilling, sandblasting, and polishing designs or lettering.

■ **Local stone shops.** Look for those specializing in kitchen countertops, tabletops, and other architectural details. These businesses are also good resources for having detail work done. They may also have remnants of stone left over from previous jobs that they would be willing to sell to you inexpensively.

■ **Stone quarries.** Look in the yellow pages for a local or possibly regional location. You might also ask local stone or monument shops about where they get their stone. Your local lumberyard or building supply center could possibly point you in the right direction for locating any stone quarries in your area.

Natural Stone

Tiles are made from granite, slate, soapstone, marble, schist, alabaster, and a dizzying array of exotic stone imported from around the world. They come in dimensioned sizes, just as their manufactured counterparts do. Because stone is a natural material, color, texture, grain patterns, and other visual effects vary from piece to piece. These variations are often considered desirable qualities, creating a unique visual effect. Stone tile can be very porous. If it doesn't come presealed, you should apply a sealant to it after installation. Also, check into getting a tile that is specially milled to have a nonskid surface for a slip-free environment.

Porcelain

Porcelain is highly refined white clay that is stamped in a mold to a desired shape and fired at an extremely high temperature. This process creates a very hard, durable, nonporous, easy-to-clean tile. Porcelain tile comes in virtually every color, design, and surface texture. It can even mimic the look of many natural stone tiles, and it's less expensive than natural stone. Instead of having a glazed finish baked onto the surface of the tile, as is the case with glazed ceramic tiles, porcelain is dyed with a pigment that carries the color through and through. Should the tile chip from abuse, there won't be any white interior blemish showing through. When purchasing a porcelain tile, stipulate to the distributor that you want through-and-through pigmented tile.

Glazed Ceramic Tile

This is a manufactured clay tile that has been machine stamped, painted with a glaze, and then

Beautiful detail work of smooth, black beach stones and blue-glazed tiles surround the oxidized bronze handles in this Maui shower.

fired in a kiln. The manufacturing process is extremely versatile, and so a wide range of textures, designs, and colors are available to choose from. The surface is hard, potentially shiny, and easy to clean. Certain types of glazed ceramic tile are manufactured with a nonskid surface that is desirable for an outdoor shower.

Terra-Cotta Tile

Typically a rustic, naturally reddish earthen tile, terra cotta is manufactured from an unrefined clay that is stamped into shape inside a mold and baked at a relatively low temperature. Like natural stone, terra cotta is porous and requires a sealant in order to protect the tile from moisture. Terra cotta is beautifully rustic, but a wet environment is not the first choice for its application.

Quarry Tile

Manufactured from red clay, quarry tile has a molded surface that resembles stone and a ridged back to aid in adhesion. Similar to terra cotta in porosity, quarry tile requires a sealant in order to be protected from mildew stains.

Mosaic Tile

Composed of many small pieces of colored terra-cotta, stone, ceramic, or porcelain tile, mosaics can be an amazing accent in any tiled environment. Literally any image can be depicted in a mosaic, and a brief investigation into traditional mosaic design uncovers a wealth of historic inspiration. Even a small mosaic flourish here and there can enhance the beauty of your outdoor shower. Given the plentitude of grout lines, slipperiness is usually not an issue for mosaics, though porosity is. A sealant should be applied over them.

Cement Tile

Cement is a very low-cost and highly effective alternative to other tile choices. It has many of the attributes of clay and ceramic tile, and it can be formed in virtually any shape, design, and color (including being pigmented throughout the entire thickness of the tile, like porcelain). However, it is extremely porous, and moisture that seeps in could lead to cracks under freezing conditions. Needless to say, a cement sealant is optimal if your shower is in a cold climate.

GOING SALVAGE

• • • • • • • • • •

Locating salvaged materials can border on a sleuthing process at times. My local salvage guy is Rodney Beauchesne. Rodney practices the age-old art of dismantling old buildings, dwellings, and other structures, salvaging the good (sometimes great) materials, and selling them off. He has woken me up early on a Sunday morning with an enthusiastic call to run down the list of the coming week's on-sale "specials." Though I am less than enthusiastic at that moment, he has supplied me with huge quantities of glass block, rigid insulation, industrial windows, and, the most precious of all, over 3,000 board feet (914 m) of old cedar, cypress, Douglas fir, and redwood. Rodney has played an important role in my business by granting me access to materials I never could have found otherwise.

Brick

Brick is a fired ceramic product that can be used structurally or aesthetically for its simple, solid, and noble look. Brick can work very nicely in conjunction with stone and tile. Brick is rather common on the salvage market. So many industrial buildings were built using the classic red brick that it is relatively easy to locate piles of "spent" block. Sometimes the old mortar is still attached to the brick and you have to spend some time chipping it off. If you're looking around for brick, also consider calling contractors who specialize in renovations. These people deal with massive amounts of this type of material. Sometimes the brick they tear down ends up in the trash, but other times a conscientious contractor will save it for reuse.

Glass

Glass is a great material to incorporate into an environment where light is a key element. I'm referring specifically to stained glass, where backlighting of a panel casts magnificent colors into an enclosure. Stained glass can be a very personal choice, however, because of the range of colors and designs. If you'd like to incorporate stained-glass panels but don't have any in your possession, try looking in antique shops. You might also visit a craft supply store to look for do-it-yourself books that can instruct you in making your own artistic stained-glass works.

Another option is glass block, which is generally available in two forms. Glass block with an internal wavy pattern allows light to pass through unimpeded but is impossible to see through clearly, thus creating privacy for the bather. Clear glass blocks do not visually screen the bather but could be used as a "window" of sorts to frame a view that you want bathers to see when they're in the shower.

Glass blocks are a construction-grade building material that offers a fast and efficient way to create a beautiful showering enclosure. Though resilient as a material, they are glass and require a certain degree of protection once they are in their finished application. Typically these blocks are double-walled, hollow "bricks" manufactured in various square sizes, traditionally 4 and 6 inches (10 and 13 cm). By stacking them on top of one another, using adhesive mastic such as mortar or silicone caulking, you can create a permanent and waterproof structure.

OPPOSITE: Built by the author, this glass block shower enclosure is especially beautiful when illuminated at night. The blocks are affixed into the 4x4 Douglas fir frame with a cement-based product.

I've located glass block through salvage and home supply centers at a very low cost, but this is one case where salvaged materials may not be better. Salvaged glass blocks could have small fractures that aren't readily apparent, creating a potential safety issue for the person handling them. Once the fractured block is mortared in place, then moisture can weep into the interior of the block as condensation, slowly filling the block enough to shatter it in a freezing climate.

Framing the Glass

When incorporated into a wall, both glass blocks and stained-glass panels have to be secured so that they receive no pressure from any direction that could cause fracturing or damage to the structural integrity of the individual pieces. The simplest solution is to construct a wooden frame that holds the glass front to back, as well as protecting the perimeter from stress. The wooden frame can be screwed into place, so that the option exists for easy removal should a problem occur.

Concrete

This versatile material is gaining a reputation for being a cost-effective way to create large areas of finished surface. Colorful pigments can be added to the concrete mix, to warm up this traditionally utilitarian material and give it a beautiful cast. It also can be buffed smooth as it is setting up, creating a soft matte finish and eventually a silky-looking surface that is a pleasure to view and feel. You can even add to the mix ornamental aggregates such as bits of glass, quartz crystals, and other types of stones that, once the surface is smoothed and polished, are quite decorative. Another inexpensive option is to use cement and rammed earth, mixed and poured into a form with steel rebar. The finished look of this combination of materials is beautifully rustic.

Concrete can be poured into any shape, size, or form to create stairs, benches, walls, tables, counters, tubs, basins — quite literally anything you can imagine. You would be hard pressed to exhaust the creative potential of the workability of concrete. It is also one of the best deals going, as it is ultimately structural and aesthetically pleasing at the same time. Concrete can mimic a surface texture of stone, tile, or stucco. You can also install radiant heat that will warm the structural mass, making for an inviting environment.

OPPOSITE: Adobe is widely used as a building material in the Southwest, and creates a wonderfully rounded freeform shower enclosure.

Metal

Metal is a traditional building material in industrial settings but is rapidly finding its way into the heart of many domestic environments. Whether the metal is brass, bronze, copper, stainless steel, corrugated tin, or iron, an aesthetic application can be found that makes use of its unique qualities. Metal is often used in cutting-edge architectural designs, often in tandem with monolithic concrete shapes, stone, water, and plantings. It lends a look of solidity, refinement of taste, and boldness of purpose and an unequivocal feeling that you are in a fortified structure.

Metal can be a fantastic material to purchase on the salvage market, because it is ultimately strong and very affordable when sold per pound. Whether new or old, it tends to retain its structural integrity (with the exception of iron, which can rust to the point of uselessness). It also doesn't take much to create a powerful visual impact. An I-beam here, a couple of square box posts there, and you now have an outdoor shower that is an event in and of itself.

You also can locate various types of metal through steel distributors and warehouses. Steel fabricators may also be able to supply you with the various metals you require, and may be able to custom-cut shapes and sizes for you.

Stucco and Plaster

There are entire regions of our country (and the world, for that matter) in which people use stucco and plaster to build all the structures they need. These "earthen" materials effortlessly lend themselves to creating organically shaped, "human-friendly" environments. The adobe style of architecture popular in the American Southwest, for example, is wonderfully soft, rounded, smooth, and free form in appearance.

Stucco and plaster are a mixture of aggregate, binding agent, and cement. Traditionally they are surface materials applied over a structural core, such as cement blocks, rammed earth, wire lathe, sandbags, or old tires, to name but a few. Stucco is typically used on the interior or exterior of a structure, whereas plaster is used only on the interior. Stucco usually leaves a rougher surface, more textured and animated to view, whereas plaster is smoother, more polished, and clean of features.

Both stucco and plaster are easily tinted, yielding a wonderfully subtle coloring without any kind of gauche painted-on effect. They can work very nicely in conjunction with stone, brick, tile, and just about every other material I have mentioned here. They work well as bridging or transition materials and yet can easily stand on their own over large expanses.

There are many variations of these products on the market, including some low-cost products that act just like high-end stucco yet cost a fraction of the price. I would suggest a careful examination of the choices before you make your purchase.

A sun-filled minimalist shower on a hilltop in Sonoma, California, utilizes the blonde stucco of the house and wide cedar trellises to frame the distant views of orchards and vineyards.

Bamboo

Bamboo is one of the most versatile materials known to humans. It has an amazing strength for its weight, yet it remains flexible even under extreme conditions. It can grow up to 4 feet (1.2 m) a day in some tropical environments and has countless uses. In Asia it is tied together to create scaffolding against the sides of the highest skyscrapers. It's used for building houses, utensils, tools, the finest tea-serving implements, furniture, fencing, walls, gates, gutters, and on and on.

Bamboo can be set in concrete to give the mixture a structural integrity, much as steel rebar is used. It also can be erected as a lathe wall over which stucco or plaster is applied, giving a beautiful, rustic aesthetic to your shower while never compromising durability. Use bamboo staves to create a trellis above your shower, tightly lashed together as a partition wall or door, or spaced apart in an open vertical frame to give a tropical feeling to a distant view as you gaze out at the scenery.

Most building suppliers stock bamboo or will order it for you. Working with this material is not only easy but also fun, and it gives a wonderful "tropical" flavor to an outdoor shower. Better yet, plant some bamboo as a grove (see box below) and enjoy the sounds of the poles clacking together in the wind.

OPPOSITE: This Asian-style shower structure is built of woven bamboo branches attached to a wooden frame. On the outside, a 1-inch-diameter bamboo framework forms a trellis for vines to grow up.

PLANTING BAMBOO

• • • • • • • • • • • •

Bamboo is a beautiful, lush, hardy reed that grows throughout the world in a wide range of climates. Growing up to 100 feet (31 m) tall and 9 inches (23 cm) in diameter throughout tropical regions, some species can thrive in weather as cold as −20°F (−28°C). Bamboo creates a soft, bushy screen, giving privacy and a poetic mood to any environment it inhabits.

There are two types of bamboo: running and clumping. A major word of caution about running varieties: they can spread very quickly. In a year or two, your little patch could be moving on to claim your entire yard. In contrast to running varieties, noninvasive clumping species of bamboo have culms that grow close together and remain in the general area in which they're planted, growing only a few inches per year. They create discrete "bushes" that accentuate the beauty and softness of your yard.

The Esalen Institute

Big Sur, California

THE ESALEN INSTITUTE IS A NONPROFIT EDUCATIONAL FOUNDATION and retreat center founded on the site of a geothermal sulfur hot springs. The institute's international clientele come to bathe, relax, attend seminars on personal growth and social change, and eat incredible food grown on-site in organic gardens.

The institute's cliffside shower room is truly extraordinary: it harnesses the sulfur water for bathers to enjoy under multiple showerheads, and sliding open the thick glass doors reveals the kelp-filled pounding surf below. The gorgeous, craggy, cliff-faced coastline runs in either direction from the shower room, setting the scene for this healing spa.

The showers at Esalen are made of cast concrete; the construction team needed six months merely to stabilize the cliff wall with long steel rods to support the structure. The shower-room walls bear the rustically refined aesthetic of concrete, fresh from the wooden forms that were used to hold it as it cured, while the pigmented floor strikes a close resemblance to oversize tile. The elements in play are quite dynamic and, short of the crashing surf below, could be recreated in a similar fashion in a domestic setting.

OPPOSITE: The cast concrete shower at the Esalen Institute offers a stunning view of the California coastline. In times of inclement weather, bathers can close the heavy glass doors.

ABOVE: Oxidized copper plumbing has a rustic appeal in this seaside shower.

OPPOSITE: Weathered white-cedar shingles, arranged in intricate patterns, adorn the exterior of this outdoor shower on Martha's Vineyard.

CHAPTER 3

Permanent Outdoor Showers

· · · · · · · · · · · · ·

THERE IS AN INFINITE NUMBER OF STRUCTURES and systems bearing the title of outdoor shower. One way to categorize them is by how they'll be used. Some are built in a permanent location and are intended to be used daily; others are set up seasonally, while still others are portable and easily carried along on a camping trip. The key aspect for you to decide is how you are going to use your shower, how permanent it will be, and how much energy you want to put into building it. Once you've determined that, you can proceed with the details of design and construction.

In general, permanent outdoor showers fit into several categories based on their proximity to a main dwelling and the amount of enclosure they have: the minimalist shower, the enclosed/attached shower, the semi-detached shower, and the fully detached shower.

All these showers are built in conjunction with a larger structure, such as a house. Either they're attached to the larger structure in some way, making use of an exterior wall as part of their own structure, or they reside in relatively close proximity to it — within 150 feet (45.7 m). These showers rely on the plumbing system of the larger structure to provide at least cold water but most often hot as well.

Any of these shower styles could be incorporated into the aesthetic of the local architectural vernacular, lending an accent of its own. A permanent outdoor shower carefully envisioned and built into your living environment can completely change the way you relate to and interact with your home.

A multi-head, minimalist beachside shower offers beachgoers a quick, one-temperature rinse.

The Minimalist Shower

This understated shower design is mainly concerned with function over form, though including even the barest essential of design elements can make it aesthetically pleasing, as well. Such a shower typically has just two control handles on the side of a wall (or as part of a freestanding design) with a showerhead projecting out over them. No enclosure separates the bathing area from the surrounding environment.

Minimalist showers are often located on a secluded back wall or section of a building, lending privacy through location, with no structural screening. The wide-open design allows bathers to have a sense of being completely free to move about as they like, while enjoying an unobstructed view of their surroundings. Simple showers like these can also be situated in remote locations, with the plumbing and hardware mounted on a pedestal of wood, bamboo, concrete, or the like. The permanent remote minimalist shower can be supplied from buried water lines or, in simpler situations, merely two garden hoses that get drained and stored for the winter.

The beauty of these showers is in the simplicity of their design. The understatement of form often means that the plumbing and fixtures bear the weight of the aesthetic focus. Some of the most common examples of minimalist showers, however, are more functional than aesthetic. Often found on public beaches, these facilities are designed for public use and give sun worshippers and bathers push-button access to an ambient-temperature freshwater shower. Rinsing off after swimming is an asset to any waterfront community, and the showering area can become a natural gathering place for people to socialize.

These public showers are built and maintained by local and state authorities, yet the designs can easily be replicated in your own yard. A simple poolside shower, for example, will allow swimmers to rinse chlorine, bromine, and any other pool chemicals from your skin, as well as simply being a refreshing place to cool down in the sun.

Of all the permanently installed outdoor shower designs, the minimalist shower is by far the least complex and least expensive to build. The basic components are the plumbing (a piped source of water, one or two temperature-control handles, a showerhead, and a drainage system), a structure to support the plumbing, and a stable surface for bathers to stand on while showering.

Minimalist Showers

What makes a shower? At its bare minimum, only the simplest elements are required: a showerhead and a way to turn on the water. Because of its simplicity, the minimalist shower can be built in any number of different settings, using a variety of materials.

ABOVE: A minimalist shower can be simply attached to the side of a house.

RIGHT: Two handles and a water-saving showerhead project out of a stucco wall. Distant views of the ocean complete the scene beautifully.

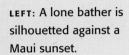

LEFT: A lone bather is silhouetted against a Maui sunset.

BELOW: This pondside cottage located on Martha's Vineyard features a private shower on the backside of the house.

ABOVE: The mermaid shower at the Kahua Hawaiian Institute shows that simple can also be whimsical.

ABOVE: Massive stone slabs and huge wooden timbers comprise this New Hampshire mountaintop shower.

RIGHT: A surfer takes advantage of this beachside shower to rinse himself (and his surfboard).

BELOW: A simple semi-permanent shower is attached to a tree. Seasonal plumbing is supplied by two garden hoses run directly out of a nearby basement window.

Freestanding

The plumbing for a minimalist shower is easily installed on a freestanding pedestal, tree, large boulder, or quite literally anything that offers a firm enough foundation. There are a number of fine commercial pedestal products to choose from in a range of materials, including wood, chrome, and stainless steel. (Many are available through specialty suppliers; see the resources.) You also could build an outdoor shower reminiscent of those found at public beaches, casting concrete in a form of your own design or using a combination of other building materials. A pedestal with two, three, or four showerheads for high-volume use is great if your pool is the site of frequent group parties or swimming functions.

Attached

If the shower is sited on the wall of a building, the plumbing can be run through the interior of the structure, hiding it completely, or can be surface mounted, thus making use of the copper pipe decoratively. I've seen examples of both approaches, and they work equally well functionally and aesthetically.

Although it will have better air circulation and will dry faster than an enclosed/attached shower, the exterior area of a building that hosts a minimalist outdoor shower should also have some degree of moisture protection included in the design and construction (see page 79). There will still be a considerable amount of water coming in contact with the exterior surface of the building, with the potential for moisture build-up and rot.

Copper, bronze, and white cedar shingles all develop a characteristic patina as they age.

The Enclosed/Attached Shower

Simply put, an enclosed/attached shower is a minimalist shower installed against the side of a building inside an enclosure. The enclosure sets the stage for privacy, thus allowing you to locate this shower anywhere you desire — even next to the front door of the house! This design style also opens up the options for including a dressing room and other ancillary spaces.

The enclosed/attached shower lends itself to every conceivable design and material combination. It can be an aesthetic statement and stand out in contrast to the building it is adjacent to, or it can blend in seamlessly with its surroundings. The range of materials you can use to construct the enclosure is vast, including all the possibilities we explored in chapter 2 (see page 40).

Often the shower's surroundings influence the design of the enclosure. For instance, many showers in coastal New England follow the style of Cape Cod vernacular — white-cedar shingles that have weathered to a soft gray, with bare or painted wooden trim. In much of the Southwest, stucco and adobe are preferred building materials for both home and shower. A deliciously pigmented stucco surface applied over a masonry core allows the design to incorporate the soft undulations of line and form that typify this style of building. The vast, open sky above and the rolling earth below inspire the use of this material. It brings the home — and shower — into context with the environment.

Protecting Against Moisture Damage

Regardless of the material you choose, there are some key construction details to bear in mind when building an enclosed/attached shower, to prevent potential water-related problems.

Protecting Your Home's Exterior First is the issue of waterproofing the wall of the house to which the shower will be attached. House exteriors are normally built to shed water, but if an outdoor shower encloses a section of wall, moisture can build up there over the years, and extra measures must be taken to keep the area from rotting. If you are building a new home and have the luxury of incorporating the shower into your overall plan, then including all the necessary layers of structural waterproofing will be convenient. If the shower is an add-on to a preexisting building, other options for waterproofing exist.

Beneath their exterior siding (whether that is wooden shingles or clapboards, vinyl, or brick), most homes are wrapped in a vapor barrier that allows moisture inside the structure to work its way out but doesn't allow exterior moisture to enter. The barrier might be tar paper in older buildings or Tyvek paper in newer ones. The vapor barrier also helps keep drafts from penetrating the walls and roof. Below this vapor barrier is an underlayment (typically some kind of plywood) that provides support for the finish siding on the exterior of the building. If you can access this layer, install marine-grade or pressure-treated plywood as the underlayment where the shower will be sited, to ensure against water damage.

To protect your house from water damage, the wall where an outdoor shower will be installed should be built (or retrofitted) with a layer of marine-grade plywood under a vapor barrier before siding is installed.

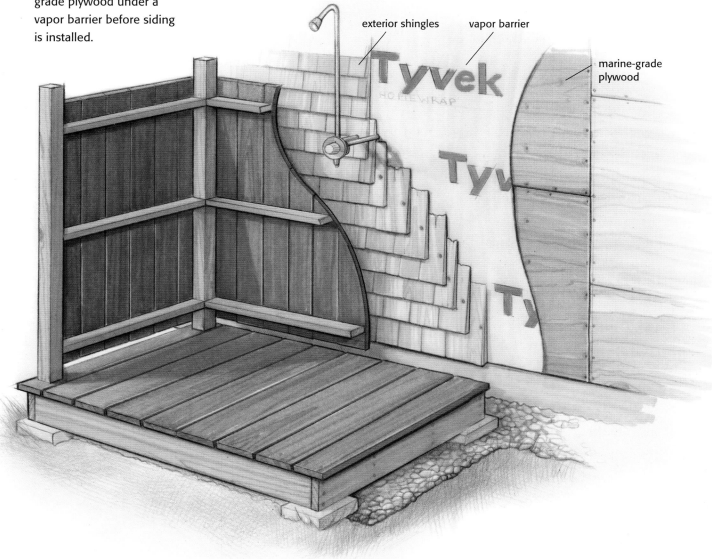

exterior shingles   vapor barrier

marine-grade plywood

If you aren't able to access the underlayment, you'll have to rely on the house's siding to prevent water from penetrating the exterior wall and causing rot. If your shower is on the south side of the building, the issue of moisture retention may not pose a problem, as it will be exposed to a good deal of sunlight. Showers facing other directions, especially the north, may be more problematic. One option to reduce the constant barrage of moisture is to construct a partition between the shower and the exterior wall, to shed the majority of the water. The partition could be made of the same material as the rest of the shower walls.

Evacuating Graywater Second is the issue of keeping the wastewater from your shower away from the foundation of your house. You'll need to take steps to ensure that the floor is well drained and that graywater is channeled away from the house. Many outdoor showers have no drainage system to speak of and simply allow the graywater to fall to the earth and eventually seep in or trickle away. For water drainage in enclosed/attached showers, however, I recommend installing either a dry well or a shower pan that directs the graywater to your household wastewater system. This way, the graywater will spend no time on the soil surface, where it can serve as a breeding ground for insects or cause rot at ground level. See chapter 1 for more details.

Ensuring Privacy

Depending on the degree of privacy you want for your shower, keep in mind when designing your enclosed/attached shower that second-story windows could potentially have a bird's-eye view into a shower that is positioned against the side of your house. So either place the shower so that it's not in the line of sight or install some kind of overhead arbor. This could even support some flowering vines that, in addition to providing privacy, would contribute to the ambience of the shower.

As for privacy from other areas of the surrounding environment, check on the angles of view and sightlines from both the interior of the shower facing out and the exterior looking in. Also avoid siting the shower in areas of unobstructed view that may make modest bathers self-conscious.

Enclosed/Attached Showers

Because of the convenience of connecting an outdoor shower into the household plumbing system, many homeowners are likely to build an enclosed/attached shower. This is simply a minimalist shower against the side of a building, with the privacy of an enclosure added.

Mahogany grillwork and an overhead arbor provide support for a privacy screen of flowering vines during the summer. Simple polished chrome pipes and a ceramic showerhead complete this attractive alcove.

ABOVE: A nautilus-shaped enclosure offers plenty of privacy from ground level, but be aware of the sight-lines from the second story of a house.

RIGHT: This deck-side shower offers a modicum of privacy from a narrow, shingled partition.

ABOVE: The shower at this guest cabin in Philo, California, is constructed of corrugated galvanized-metal panels and pressure-treated framing.

LEFT: This simple shower has two doors for complete privacy and a generous showerhead.

RIGHT: Located next to a granite slab with a carved foot-rinsing basin, this Martha's Vineyard shower features a pyramid-shaped arbor above.

OPPOSITE: A circular semi-detached shower provides plenty of privacy, despite its location by the front entrance of this home.

The Semi-Detached Shower

The semi-detached outdoor shower is a self-contained shower room sited away from the main building but connected to it by a breezeway, trellis, fence, free-standing wall, or section of roof or deck. Building your shower in this fashion will give it an element of spaciousness and independence of form from its surrounding architecture. The shower stands on its own, offering you a unique vantage point from which to experience your surroundings, as well as a sense of going on an adventure.

The design of the semi-detached shower bridges the attributes of the enclosed/attached and the fully detached showers. It's a compromise of moving the shower away from a structurally supportive wall, yet not entirely letting go into an independent location; it creates a human-scale space with a distinct personality. It can also accentuate an aspect of the surrounding environment, while blending in with the overall architectural design of your house and outbuildings.

This combination of relationships between structures opens up a plethora of design possibilities. I've come across a number of semi-detached showers that use a variety of materials in very imaginative ways. The materials chosen for the shower don't have to be the same as those used on the main building in order to achieve an architecturally harmonious design. The circular semi-detached shower on the opposite page fits in well with its surroundings, both because of the building material and because of its use as a gradual transition between the driveway and the entrance to the house.

Structurally, the semi-detached shower is simply an enclosed shower set away from the main building. The plumbing for this style of shower is similar to that of the enclosed/attached shower. Instead of connecting to the shower through an exterior wall of the main building, however, the hot and cold lines are typically run from the house to the shower under the deck, through a low partition, or in an overhead structural canopy.

Drainage is handled in the same way as for the enclosed/attached shower. A dry well can be dug and filled with gravel to instantly disperse the graywater into the ground. Alternatively, a shower pan can be installed beneath the shower floor to evacuate the water to the surrounding landscape or to the household septic line.

Semi-Detached Showers

Semi-detached showers bear some structural relationship to the house but are not constructed directly against it. Often they are connected to a dwelling by a deck, overhead trellis, or breezeway. The shower's style and building materials may or may not relate to those of the house.

LEFT: The curved face of this shower offers a gradual transition from the driveway to the house.

BELOW: An overhead trellis and multiple showerheads create an open and accessible backyard shower.

RIGHT: The use of stone and wood in this shower complements the building style of the main house.

The Fully Detached Shower

The monarch of the outdoor shower family exists away from any physical or aesthetic connection to surrounding structures, becoming something of a destination in the yard, the site of a daily showering pilgrimage. This design allows the bather privacy and seclusion and promotes a contemplative attitude toward life. Depending on your intention, your shower can be virtually hidden with a natural screen of living camouflage, or it can make a strong aesthetic statement by drawing attention to its design.

By capitalizing on the element of seclusion, your fully detached outdoor shower can also provide you with an incredibly rare experience: the sensation of being in a foreign and exotic land, far from the day-to-day world you're used to. The feeling is akin to that of the creative child who builds hidden forts and magical secret playhouses. A meandering pathway can lead to your private sanctuary, set against a natural backdrop of your favorite plantings.

This style of shower leaves the options wide open for exploring just how creative you can be. Some of the detached showers I've seen were intended to make the most of gorgeous surrounding daytime views, while others — particularly those with well-placed ambient lighting — are best used in darkness, luring a bather out for a refreshing nighttime rinse.

Walkway to the Shower

A key element of the detached outdoor shower is the pathway leading out to it. I recommend carefully mapping out the best route to your detached shower and laying down a pathway of a durable, level material. The subtly uneven footing in a yard can become tenuous at best when you are wrapped in a towel, barefoot, walking in the dark, and carrying an armful of toiletries. Having stable, even footing while you navigate the route to an outdoor shower creates a seamless transition into your bathing environment.

OPPOSITE: Made of durable bamboo, plexiglass panels, and a thatched roof, this Maui shower offers a relaxing bathing area even during tumultuous winter storms.

LEFT: A well-laid brick path makes the walkway to and from the shower a safe and pleasant experience, day or night.

Fully Detached Showers

For the true outdoor shower enthusiast, the fully detached shower, set away from any other structure, offers the bather the experience of going on an adventure. These showers are best when they look like a part of their site and take advantage of surrounding views.

LEFT: Large basalt stones are set into a bed of mortar to form the pathway to this fully detached shower.

BELOW: Perennials and small shrubs help this garden shower blend into the rest of the landscape.

RIGHT: Long concrete slabs guide the bather to this secluded shower in Benson, Arizona.

In some cases, a grassy path may be all you need (although it can be annoying to have your feet get covered with freshly mown clippings on your way back to the house). Slate slabs, flat blocks of cut granite, or bricks fitted tightly together also fit the bill nicely. Stone pavers create a rustic, cobbled effect and offer the opportunity to plant moss in the spaces between the blocks. Stones and bricks can shift and heave, however, if they're not bedded in a layer of pulverized peastone or gravel.

Wooden planking is also appropriate under certain circumstances. However, don't just set the wood on the earth, because eventually even the most rot-resistant woods will absorb water and rot. Instead, use cement blocks or stones to create elevated platforms on which you can set the wooden planking.

Splinters, though, are a real and nasty threat to tender feet. If wood is your preferred choice for a walkway, I suggest you use a dense, tight-grained softwood like Port Orford cedar or Douglas fir. These woods are often used as decking, and if sanded smooth and coated with a clear preservative, they will remain splinter free.

Bluestone pavers set into grass make a comfortable, nonslippery path to and from a fully detached shower.

Fallen plant material can also give the bather an uncomfortable walking experience. A friend of mine has a shower located near a holly tree, and on more than one unfortunate occasion I have been impaled on spiky holly leaves lying in the grass. My association with that shower carries with it memories of pain. A slightly raised walkway that is easily swept off would do away with any of these unpleasant conditions.

If your detached shower will be used primarily at night, be sure to also give some thought to lighting the way. Creating a well-lighted pathway is an essential aspect for everyone's safety and comfort. See chapter 1 for more information on lighting.

Plumbing Considerations

Practically speaking, the plumbing elements of this shower are the same as those of attached and semi-detached showers; the pipes simply run a greater distance. If your detached shower is more than 75 feet (23 m) from a preexisting hot water supply (such as that of your house), it's wise to install an on-demand hot water heater near your shower. You'll need to build a small enclosure near the shower site to house the heater, and you'll need to make accommodations for powering it. If the heater is electric, you'll need to run electricity out to the shower site. If it burns propane, you'll need to run a propane line from your house or install a propane tank next to your shower.

To get the water out to a remote detached shower, ¾-inch (19 mm) copper pipe is the rule. It should be buried at least 12 inches (31 cm) below grade in a bed of clean sand, with no rocks. If you live in a region that freezes during the winter, the water supply lines will need to have an extension that is pitched to an access hole and terminates in a removable plug, so that you can drain the pipes before freezing temperatures set in.

Fully detached outdoor showers usually drain into their own dry well. However, you may want to make the most of the resulting graywater from your shower by using it to irrigate surrounding landscape plants. This can be accomplished very simply by installing a shower pan that directs water to nearby gardens. Alternatively, you could create a shower floor of poured concrete that's pitched slightly outward, so that the graywater can run off directly into the surrounding soil.

The Indoor-Outdoor Shower

Technically speaking, these are not true outdoor showers, in the sense of being sited outside the house. Instead, these showers are to be found inside, usually attached to a master bedroom; if they're near an outside wall, a door close at hand may offer bathers the ability to stroll outside after a relaxing shower.

Though not sited entirely outdoors, the indoor-outdoor shower contains certain qualities that set it apart from the standard indoor shower. Typically this type of shower is not contained in an enclosure, and if it is, the space allocated to showering is voluminous. Often the shower is part of an open bathroom floor plan that utilizes a central drain to evacuate the water. Keeping the bathroom dry is not necessarily the focus in this type of situation. The floor and walls are often finished with tile, and the ceiling is finished with more tile or with marine-grade paint. Because the environment is capable of withstanding a free flow of water, the bather is able to move around in this space without giving a thought to water-damage issues.

Indoor-outdoor showers offer many design options. The bathing area can be at the same floor level as the rest of the room, with the floor of the entire room gently sloping down to a drain. Alternatively, it could step down significantly into a short enclosure, sort of an open walk-in tub for showering, with its own drain. Another option is to set the shower at floor level but enclose it with a slightly raised perimeter, perhaps a 6-inch (15 cm) wall, which contains most of the water on the floor immediately around the bather. The shower is open and allows plenty of room for bathers to move around, yet it is set within clearly defined boundaries.

In cases where privacy is a consideration, a partition separating the shower from the rest of the bathroom may be necessary. Semitransparent materials like glass block are ideal in this scenario. Outdoors or in, glass block is a fantastic material for creating walls, partitions, and enclosures. Clear enough to allow light to pass through unimpeded, yet obscured enough to prevent anyone from seeing through them, glass blocks allow bathers to feel naturally illuminated while remaining in privacy.

Indoor-Outdoor Showers

Although not sited outdoors, this style of shower usually has some kind of easy access to the outside. The indoor-outdoor shower also offers the bather an opportunity to shower in an unenclosed interior environment — typically in a large, open space finished with materials that can be exposed to water.

ABOVE: These translucent glass blocks simultaneously provide bathers with light and privacy.

LEFT: Foliage from indoor plants provides the bather with additional privacy in this indoor-outdoor shower.

ABOVE: This Japanese-style soaking tub and shower, built by the author, combine Alaskan yellow cedar, western red cedar, and slate.

RIGHT: Stucco and green slate cover the walls of this pool shower in Tucson, Arizona.

The White Lotus Retreat Center

Santa Barbara, California

THIS YOGA AND SPIRITUAL RETREAT CENTER, located in the San Marcos Pass, east of Santa Barbara, features the quintessential minimalist outdoor shower. Utilizing two enormous side-by-side boulders that were already on site, the owners installed copper water lines that run underneath and then up and over the top to a basin between the stones. The water comes cascading down in a waterfall onto the reveling bather below. Two temperature-control handles are conveniently located at waist height, and the temperature of the waterfall can be micro-adjusted to suit individual taste. To complete this astounding shower feature, the owners laid a mosaic tile floor complete with a center drain. The shower has a stunning view out over the Coast Range and Pacific Ocean.

OPPOSITE: The waterfall shower combines the comfort of a hot shower with the beauty of bathing in nature.

ABOVE: A plastic trash can harvests rainwater for a gravity-fed shower.

OPPOSITE: Outdoor showers need not be complicated to set up. This one, attached to a white oak, is supplied with both hot and cold water from two garden hoses that are disconnected at the end of the season.

CHAPTER 4

Temporary Showers

• • • • • • • • • • • • • •

HERE IS WHERE WE PART WAYS WITH THE WORLD of permanent shower installation. Temporary showers are motivated by a different set of bathing requirements (usually ease of assembly and use) and thus require a different approach to construction. The kind of temporary shower you create is dependent on how and where you'll be using it, as well as how portable it must be. For instance, a camp shower that needs to be taken apart and packed up every day or two will require a different setup than a shower that will be used by a group of people at a weeklong music festival.

The Solar Shower

If you're hiking and want to have a means of washing with hot water somewhat consistently, you'll most likely want a solar shower. This is a reinforced black plastic bag that holds up to 5 gallons (19 L) of water and is fitted with a "watering can" style of nozzle. You hang the black bag from a nearby tree branch, where it absorbs the heat of the sun, warming the water inside. When you're ready to shower, you simply open a valve near the showerhead, and out comes the water. Such a shower feels extravagant in rustic conditions. When empty and rolled up for traveling, the entire apparatus weighs no more than a few ounces.

A typical solar shower set-up. The black plastic bag is filled with water and heats up in the sun while hanging from the apex of a tripod (which can be wrapped with a tarp for privacy). The pallet keeps the bather off the ground and out of wet soil or mud.

There are many solar shower products on the market to choose from (see the resources). The drawback is that if there isn't any sun, you don't get a hot shower. There are ways to overcome that obstacle, however, such as heating water on a camp stove or fire and mixing in enough cold water to create the desired temperature for your solar shower. (Always put the cold water in your bag first, and then add the hot. If you do it the other way around, the bag may melt.)

Whatever the conditions you're faced with while hiking or camping, the solar shower may well be your salvation, considering the bulk and weight of other shower systems.

The Fixed-Location Camp Shower

Here is a horse of a different color. With the ability to drive in all the supplies you need comes greater flexibility in creating your outdoor shower. Material weight is no longer of consequence, so the type of temporary shower you build is dictated only by your needs and the degree of imagination you want to bring to the design.

The required components for this shower are a structural framework that provides support for the plumbing and any enclosure you might want, a system for heating the water, a pump (either electric or manual) that delivers the water to the showerhead, a platform for the bather to stand on, a showerhead and temperature-control handles, and a graywater drainage system.

Structure

Camp showers usually employ a relatively solid structure for an ongoing period of time. Typically they're used for a week or two, though an extended camping sojourn could easily keep them in operation for months at a time. The use of a semipermanent plumbing material such as CPVC tubing (see chapter 1) guarantees that smooth operation will continue indefinitely as long as you have taken care to assemble all the joints and fixtures securely.

The physical framework of the camp shower can be assembled with a variety of materials that easily affix to one another and just as easily disassemble — 2x4 wood framing stock or plywood secured with screws or carriage bolts, tree saplings bound together with rope, metal conduit with angle brackets, and inevitably a host of other materials.

Presize the materials at home to make sure that everything fits together well and is ready for efficient on-site assembly. You can label all the parts so that you can set up the shower without a hitch when your reach your destination. The initial investment you make in designing and prefabricating your shower will make the reassembly easy to perform with a few hand tools, such as a hammer, cordless screw gun, and pliers.

Water Supply

Where your water comes from will depend, in some part, on how far away from civilization you're constructing your shower. You might need to pump or haul water from a nearby pond, lake, or stream. In areas that receive rain reliably, you might consider setting up a rain catchment. Purchasing water from a local tanker truck is sometimes a possibility. If you're near enough a water spigot, you might just hook up your shower to it with a garden hose.

Heating the Water

The temporary shower, like any other shower, works by drawing heated water overhead and controlling the volume as it descends over the bather's body. If you want to take advantage of mechanizing your shower, you can use a propane burner to flash-heat your water in a metal container. Manually mix in cold water to balance it, and use a small electric motor to siphon this "shower-ready" mix to the showerhead with the flick of a switch.

If you don't want the responsibility of electric motors, you can use a standard marine foot pump to transfer the water from the mixing container up to a hanging reservoir above the bather. Once the water is in place, opening a release valve will allow it to exit the container via an attached showerhead.

Dealing with Graywater

You can construct a simple platform by attaching a series of boards side by side to two crosspieces beneath them. The boards on top of the platform should have spaces between them to allow water to drain through. The platform gets the bather off the ground, provides a stable surface to stand on, and allows the graywater to drain from the bathing platform. If the soil beneath the platform has a sufficient percolation rate, you can allow the graywater to simply fall to the ground and be absorbed into the earth. Otherwise, install a watertight pan under

In addition to its unique shape, the Entomo shower has a sophisticated graywater filtering system. It collects all the wastewater from the shower and sends it through a series of five filters to remove impurities before returning it to the surrounding soil.

the platform to collect the graywater, and pipe it to a better spot (downhill) for absorption into the earth.

Digging a dry well and filling it with gravel is most likely unrealistic for the conditions under which this style of shower is implemented. I recommend taking the time to figure out how to dispose of the graywater responsibly, though, because a concentration of soaps, shampoos, and other complex chemical compounds can have a damaging effect on the environment if they drain directly into open bodies of water or are allowed to become concentrated in one spot.

The Entomo Shower

A good example of a temporary shower that's both imaginative and environmentally sensitive is the Entomo shower, designed and built by mechanical engineer Jonathan West. True to its entomological name, the shower is shaped like a giant wasp, and each body part has a different function.

The water for this shower is purchased from a tanker supply truck and stored in a 55-gallon (208 L) barrel. Mounted inside the barrel is an electric pump that sends the water up the interior of a leg and into the abdomen of this fabricated metal insect shower. The pump is activated by a spring-loaded switch in the hinge mechanism of a wooden grill platform suspended over the graywater containment pool. As bathers step onto the platform and stand under the thorax, water automatically cascades over them and is collected beneath the wooden grill for recycling.

The graywater is pumped from the containment pool through a series of four filters. The first filter is a fine mesh that traps relatively large solids. Following is a sand trap and then a heavy-duty filter that removes particles down to 20 microns in size. Finally, a carbon filter collects particles down to 5 microns in size. West uses the cleaned and filtered graywater to hose down the area around the camp. He takes the collected sludge and dumps it in a landfill in a nearby town. The filters can store up to 25 pounds (11.3 kg) of silt and need cleaning only after about a week of continuous use.

The Entomo system costs about $1,500 to build. The filters need to be replaced on a yearly basis, at a cost of approximately $80. West says that he could continue to filter the graywater even further with infrared filters to create potable water, but it was a hard sell to his friends.

MANUAL OR ELECTRIC?

Depending on your situation, outdoor showers can be either manually operated or powered by electricity. A shower run purely on muscle power is simple to build and easy to maintain or repair, especially when just a few people will be using it. However, with the utilization of electric or gas-powered devices, some operations become more efficient. Large volumes of water for many people can be pumped and processed in a fraction of the time needed to work by hand.

There is a downside to this kind of high-tech approach, though. Machines with complex moving parts require maintenance and are liable to break down. If you're not mechanically inclined, or if you're building a shower out in the wilderness (where spare machine parts or a mechanic are nigh on impossible to find), you may want to opt for a manual system. Fewer working parts to break down mean less to fix.

Also consider the environmental impact of whichever system you choose. Gas-powered pumps, for instance, discharge carbon monoxide as exhaust, not only polluting the air, but also detracting considerably from the ambience of your outdoor shower.

THE LOW-IMPACT, MANUALLY OPERATED SHOWER

This design is easy to assemble and requires only minimal materials. The flow of water is controlled by the bather as required.

- A source for heating the water, such as propane burner and tank

- A 5-gallon (19 liter) metal pot for heating and mixing water

- A foot-operated nautical bilge pump

- A tripod made out of three 8-foot (2.4 m) lengths of 2-inch (5 cm) schedule 40 PVC or 2-inch (5 cm) aluminum pipe joined at the top by carriage bolts

- 16 feet (4.9 m) of I-inch (19 mm) heat-resistant, flexible, nautical-grade hose

- A 3-foot by 3-foot (91 cm by 91 cm) wooden grill-work platform, such as a pallet

- A showerhead

Begin by erecting the tripod; the bases of the legs should be 4 to 5 feet from each other. Place the wooden platform on the ground below the apex of the tripod. For privacy, wrap a tarp around the outside of the tripod, covering the first 6 vertical feet or so (remember to leave an entry/exit flap).

Attach the showerhead with wire to the apex of the tripod and run the feed tube down one of the legs, winding it around the leg several times to keep it out of the bathing space. Insert the end of the feed tube into the foot-operated pump, and set the pump on the platform.

Place the propane tank and burner near the platform, within reach of the pump. Open the valve on the propane tank and light the burner. Fill the metal pot with 3 gallons of water and set it on the burner to heat. When the water is fully heated, mix in enough cold water to reach a suitable temperature for showering.

Run a length of hose from the intake of the foot-operated pump to the pot on top of the burner, and insert the end of the hose into the heated water (you may need to tie or clamp it to the edge of the pot so that it won't fall out). Step onto the platform, and start pumping. The water will be siphoned into the hose and up to the showerhead. Five gallons of water, if used judiciously, will provide a very adequate shower.

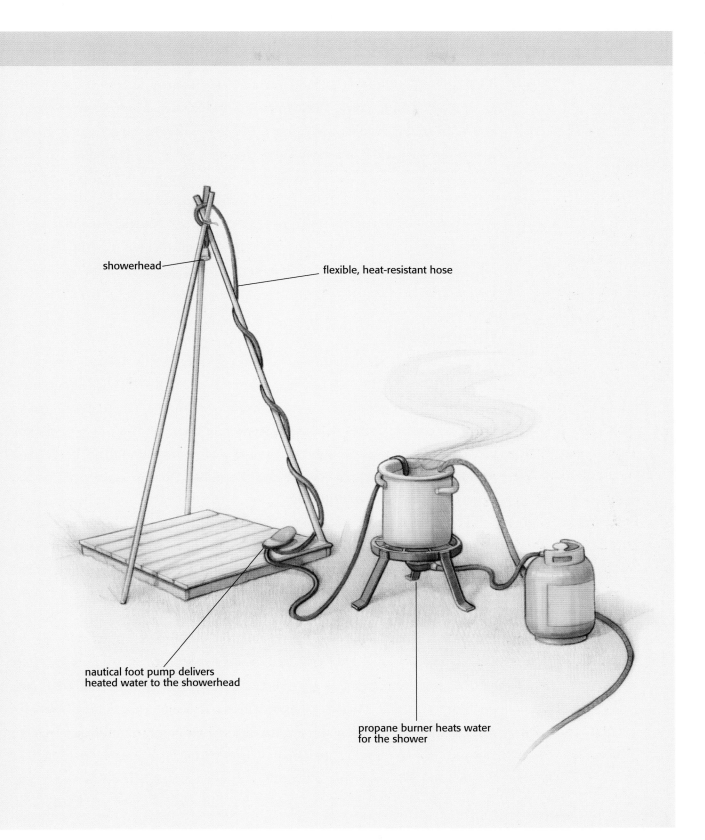

showerhead

flexible, heat-resistant hose

nautical foot pump delivers
heated water to the showerhead

propane burner heats water
for the shower

The Opportunistic Shower

This last outdoor shower category includes infinite possibilities for washing up, rinsing off, cooling down, bathing, or just getting wet. These showers exist in every climate, environment, and locale. Sometimes they are obvious, such as a fire hydrant in the middle of a city neighborhood on a sweltering summer day. This type of shower brings tremendous joy and relief to the people near it.

Opportunistic showers can be human-made devices, but most often showering was not their intended use. These showers may also be creations of nature just waiting to be discovered and appreciated by someone. Either way, the responsibility falls on your shoulders, so to speak, to search out and locate one of your own. That is the opportunistic part.

The Scoop Bath

A very common style of bathing in Southeast Asia as well as in many other subtropical and tropical regions of the world is the scoop bath. This simple bath is merely a large vessel, filled from a source of running or standing water, and a handheld container used to pour the water over the body. Men and women can be seen bathing in public in this fashion, while wearing a sarong or simple piece of cloth to retain a degree of modesty. The ambient-temperature water is used to get wet, lather up, and rinse off.

This system of bathing is quite effective in environments where private bathrooms and septic systems simply don't exist. Friends provide assistance for each other by taking turns being the "water pourer," freeing up both hands of the bather to attend to the process of washing.

The Black Hose

One ultimately simple shower for use in a warm climate on a sunny day is the black hose shower. Purchase a 50-foot (15.2 m) length of black hose from your local garden supplier, and attach a pressure nozzle to the end. Fill the hose with water and leave it in the sun. When the need arises, simply squeeze the nozzle to produce a hot shower (the duration of which will be determined by the length of the hose and the speed with which you use the water). Exercise caution when you first turn on the hose, however, because the water may be extremely hot.

Two bathers take advantage of the natural shower offered by a waterfall.

The Burning Man Festival

Black Rock, Nevada

EXQUISITE EXAMPLES OF TEMPORARY SHOWERS can be found in profusion at the Burning Man Festival, an artistic collaboration that takes place annually in the Black Rock Desert in northern Nevada. More than 35,000 participants descend on the desert, where streets and avenues are set up, and people build theme camps featuring a vast array of creative installations.

Showers make up a large part of the skyline at this festival. Because the idea is to leave no trace of human presence once the festival is over, shower creators must employ creative means to make sure that no body paint, soap, or shampoo remains. The solution that most revelers use is the evaporation pool. This consists of a wide, shallow pool in which graywater is collected and evaporated in the scorching desert sun. This is a relatively successful system — when cloudy weather doesn't prevent evaporation and dust doesn't turn the pool into a muddy mess. The typical evaporation pool consists of a 10-foot-square (0.9 sq m) sheet of clear- or black-plastic tarp laid on the ground with a square frame of PVC tubing raising the perimeter edge so that it will hold water. Once the water has evaporated, the plastic and remaining residue is disposed of in a landfill.

LEFT: A pickle-shaped showerhead at the Burning Man Festival.

OPPOSITE: Black plastic is a way to collect and dispose of soap residue once the graywater from a shower has evaporated.

ABOVE: Grinning like the Cheshire Cat, this woodland deity watches over all who pass his stone wall on the way to the shower.

OPPOSITE: This formal enclosed shower ensures privacy amid an enclave of buildings.

CHAPTER 5

Planning and Design

• • • • • • • • • • • •

IN ORDER TO SUCCESSFULLY REALIZE YOUR DREAM of creating an outdoor shower, you must begin with an overall plan that will guide you through the different stages of the project. You're likely to find that your initial projections about location, design, and budget, to name but a few, are not entirely accurate or practical. This is typical of most construction projects and should not be a cause for concern. It is important to maintain flexibility throughout the planning and building process; your work may unveil unexpected opportunities, allowing for fresh inspiration that can benefit all aspects of the project.

Instead of having a contractor design your shower, you may decide that you want to do it yourself. Hopefully, by reading the first part of this book, you've become familiar with the wide variety

of style and design options that can be used as inspiration. Possibly you already have a clear idea of what you want and are primed to implement the construction phase right off. Or perhaps you're still in the pre-design stage. Whatever your present situation is, bring what you have to the process and explore the myriad elements that will see your shower through to completion.

OPPOSITE: The south-facing deck of this cabin on Martha's Vineyard offers the perfect spot for an outdoor shower to be installed.

Budget and Schedule

A very important first step is to determine what you're willing to spend on your shower, and then to contemplate what, if any, leeway you have in amending this number. The actual costs of projects commonly run over what initial projections establish, and vast overruns can turn a project into an extremely unsavory situation. So closely examine what your budget parameters are, and keep them in mind when making decisions about your outdoor shower project.

Another key element in the initial planning stage, but one that can be difficult to realistically pin down, is the timeline. If you're working with a contractor, he or she should be able to give you a rough estimate. Even after 20 years of building, however, I sometimes underestimate the amount of time each detail will require. When the projects I'm contracted for involve new mechanical and aesthetic challenges, I'm not able to take advantage of the efficiency of motion and experiential knowledge that comes from repetitive practice. In these cases, doubling, tripling, or even quadrupling what seems to be the most reasonable initial schedule projection brings it closer to the final reality. Once the elements of your design and your choice of materials start to gel, it becomes easier to project how long the project "should" take.

Creating a Budget

Just like any construction project, the budget for your outdoor shower will comprise three costs: design, materials, and labor. Estimating your financial outlay will depend on how much of the project you want to do yourself. If you're hiring someone for either the design or construction portions of the project (see, "Finding a Good Contractor," page 120), he or she will be responsible for calculating costs and should present you with an estimate before the project gets underway.

If you're taking on the designing and/or building yourself, the following are some guidelines to help you make a budget for materials. Begin by dividing your project into phases, and make a list of all of the materials and tools you imagine will be necessary to carry out each phase. The key to making a complete materials list is thinking about each phase as if you're actually building it. For example, consider the site preparation as one phase. What will that involve? Will you have to rent a backhoe to dig the foundation, or is it small enough to dig by hand? If you're digging a dry well, how many yards of gravel will you need to have delivered?

You can then estimate the costs of individual materials by researching online, or simply by calling around to various suppliers. It's important to get quotes from a number of different sources, as prices can vary widely.

Finding a Good Contractor

If you want to hire a professional contractor to oversee the construction of your outdoor shower, there are certain guidelines you should follow for locating, hiring, and working with this person. Contractors are trained and licensed to carry out all facets of construction. They usually do some of the hands-on work themselves and farm out certain tasks to subcontractors, either to speed up the project or because the task involves work outside the scope of their expertise (for example, a building contractor might subcontract with a plumber to install the water supply and drainage system). As the client, you should at least feel comfortable with and trusting of, if not downright excited and enthusiastic about, your choice of contractor.

Locating a contractor can be a real challenge if you are starting off cold. One of the best ways to find a fair, reliable, hardworking contractor who produces high-quality work is by word of mouth. The testimony of a trusted friend who had a good experience with a particular contractor is tremendously valuable. The time you spend up front making sure that the person you're hiring is worthy of your investment of time, energy, resources, and peace of mind is of the utmost importance. Hiring someone without sufficient references, background checks, previous client testimonials, and portfolio submissions may not only get your project off on the wrong foot but may put it on a crash-course trajectory with a disastrous conclusion. Ultimately, there is no reason to think you can save time or expense by rushing through the process of finding the right partner for your project. So be careful, and do your homework.

OPPOSITE: Douglas fir timbers create a frame for the 6-by-6-inch glass blocks that will enclose this shower.

If you have no personal recommendations from friends, find at least three contractors in your area to interview. Have an initial meeting with each of them to go over your projected requirements (such as design, budget, and timeline), and ask each for recommendations from previous clients complete with contact information, images of completed projects, a copy of their liability insurance policy, and their valid contractor license number. Contractors should be willing to furnish all of this to you, and then it is up to you to research all of this information.

Depending on how much of the shower you'd like to build yourself, you may only need to find a good plumber to install the plumbing. Most professional plumbers should be comfortable setting up the basic fixtures for a shower, but it's certainly advantageous to hire someone who has specific experience installing outdoor showers.

A flowering dogwood is the backdrop for this enclosed/attached shower. The owners chose a west-facing site, and the sunny shower is a welcome respite at the end of the day.

DREAM SHOWERS

These designs are the result of brainstorming sessions I have had with friends and family. We worked with various environments and physical challenges to see what kind of creative showering scenarios we could come up with. They may offer you an idea or set your own creative juices flowing. As you go about your own brainstorming for shower ideas, remember to stay open to the unexpected.

The Teahouse Shower

With its Japanese teahouse–inspired design, this meditation hut and outdoor shower usher in a sense of relaxation and calmness. Built on a small scale, the teahouse could serve simply as a changing area for the shower. On a larger scale, it could be the perfect setting for a weekend hideaway.

What to Expect

This initial meeting is usually free of cost, as it is just a preliminary consultation. The contractors will want to take a set of your working building plans with them in order to prepare a bid or make an estimate for the job. If you don't have a set of plans at this time, you can hire an architect to draw some (the criteria for hiring an architect are similar to those for hiring a contractor), work with your contractor to design it with you, or design it yourself (see "Design Ideas," page 126). With good working plans, you should be able to get back from your prospective contractors an accurate estimate of the price they will charge you for the construction.

Compare the estimates you get back from the contractors, but also consider your future relationship with them. You may end up hiring someone who doesn't have the lowest bid but seems to be the best overall to work with.

Once you have a design, a contractor, and a workable price, you and your contractor can work out a timeline that is acceptable for both of you. Be sure to discuss the degree of flexibility you have for the project's stretching beyond the anticipated completion date. A common mistake in homebuilding, for example, is to plan a housewarming party or moving-in day for a date soon after the projected completion of the house. As the arbitrarily chosen end date approaches and time gets short, massive pressure to finish on time can result. In the end, there may be some slipshod work as workers cut corners trying to reach a rapidly approaching goal. While it's good to know what your preferred end date is, it's also helpful to allow the contractor some flexibility for when a schedule runs behind.

Your contractor will work with you to write up a contract outlining all the key information pertaining to the services to be rendered, design expectations, payment schedules tied to certain steps of the projects, and the dates by which these stages are to be completed. Both you and your contractor should sign and date the contract, and each of you should retain a copy of it for your records.

At the end of the project is the punch list, a list of the last of the details that need to be taken care of, including all those little loose ends that make your shower a completed process. The list is merely whatever is so far left undone or fully completed on any project. Sometimes design details get changed and are put off until the end of the project to wrap up, or something breaks and needs repair, or there are scratches in the surface of a finished material that need to be fixed. Completion of the punch list details can make or break a project. If your contractor sees all of these items through (as he or she is under contract to do), then

great! Job well done. If not — and some people just somehow miss finishing all the details — then make sure to bring them to your contractor's attention. Final payment should not be made until the job is completely finished.

Design Ideas

Whether or not you decide to build your own outdoor shower, you may be inspired to design one on your own. If you have a working knowledge of design and construction, you won't be limited by the need to hire professionals to create a shower design for you. There will always be a need for skilled craftspeople to supply specialized services when they are required. But learning a bit about design can help personalize your project.

The minimalist shower at the base of this tiered sun deck is perfect for rinsing off beach sand before entering the hot tub.

Presented here are suggestions for ways to approach the design process for your outdoor shower. Depending on the style you find most comfortable to work with, take with you whatever tips are useful and allow them to guide your creative process.

Keep a Journal

I keep a collection of images (from books, magazine articles, newspaper clippings, and photos I've shot) to remind myself of the inspiring ideas of others. An old stone foundation deep in the woods, a trellis attached to a three-season lakeside pavilion, or a Balinese tree-house hotel — all such ideas should be exploited for their ability to educate the eye. Use these aesthetic features to spark your own creative drive.

Your journal should contain all the information pertinent to your design and conceptualization stage, contact information for various sources of materials, directions for locating materials you come across on your investigative adventures, pricing information, and all the random ideas, brainstorms, and suggestions that other people give you. All this information is important to keep track of because each and every step along the way is going to produce helpful information that will deepen and enrich your shower project.

Another good source of information and design ideas is the Internet. Do a search using keywords like *outdoor shower, poolside structure, pavilion, trellis, stone building and sculpture, wooden play structures,* and Inevitably you will find more information than you could possibly want, so narrow it down to what is the most relevant to your personal taste, whether it's a stone sculpture by Isamu Noguchi or a redwood trellis from a company in northern California.

This stage of the process may extend beyond your journal to include special building materials or other objects you've collected along the way. Through the years, I've collected materials that had no immediate use at the time but were so full of promise for a later project that I purchased (or bartered for) them or simply spent the time and energy to haul them off the beach or out of the woods. I store them in a garage or the basement, waiting until the right building project comes along. You, too, may have a secret stash of materials you'll want to consider for your project.

Design *In Situ*

Seasoned designers spend plenty of time in the environment they're being hired to work with. Some will take an entire year to track the seasonal changes, familiarizing themselves with the subtle transitions that affect the environment through light and temperature. The end design should be a reflection of the location, looking as if it grew out of the environment as naturally as a tree.

OPPOSITE: A framed window without glass provides the bather with a view of the surrounding environment.

Your own design will benefit from the time you spend in the space where your outdoor shower will be built. There will certainly be a time when you'll need to refine your ideas and think about the practical aspects of the shower, but for a time, allow your creativity to flow unobstructed from your rational mind.

Start by collecting some materials to draw with, such as a sketch pad, pencils, pens, oil pastel sticks, charcoal, finger paints, or whatever you find the easiest and most fun to work with. Gather your design materials and go to the location where you want to build your outdoor shower (if you are contemplating more than one site and don't yet know which is preferable, this exercise may help you decide). While you are walking, imagine what kind of path you would like to have leading to the showering environment. Do you already have stone or brick walkways on your land? Maybe you want to add a new element to your yard, something special just for the shower. Visualize the type of material as well as the feel of it under your feet. Carefully placed cobblestones? Pigmented concrete pads with aggregate in them? Bricks laid in a herringbone motif?

Next, stand in the location where you expect the showerhead to cast its water. Look around and experience the shower structure of your dreams. Is there a structure at all? Maybe it is enough just to have a simple arrangement composed of just the plumbing, without the addition of any enclosure. Or possibly you see in your mind's eye a simple room of sorts. Go through the scenarios of the different materials and options you are considering. Does the enclosure have both walls and a door? What is the material used — stone, wood, brick, or stucco? Is there an opening to look out of so you can gaze at a beautiful feature of your yard or distant view? What is over your head — a trellis of strong timbers defining the sky, possibly with a vine growing in a pleasingly serpentine fashion through it? Or is the sky view uninterrupted?

Use your imagination and really feel what it will be like to inhabit this space. Do you want room for two people to shower simultaneously? How will this factor affect the placement of the showerheads? Will there be any kind of lighting installed so that you can safely and conveniently shower at night?

As you ask yourself these questions, be open to the silent answers that come to you in the form of images or ideas. Draw what first comes to mind without thinking about it. No matter how wild or ridiculous an image may be, just let it come out and lead you on to the next one. You are working with the influence of the space here, and inevitably it has a lot to offer. You may suddenly understand

something about the location that never dawned on you before. Or you might realize that it is better to slightly change the location to a spot that is better suited to your taste. Or maybe carefully changing the orientation to a different direction would make all the difference.

The final structure may end up looking nothing like the images you're dreaming up here, but this is a very important step in the process. All other designs will follow these first loose, wild, inspired sketches.

The creators of this simple outdoor shower have used a black locust branch to add an organic flair and give the morning glories something to climb.

Tree-House Shower

The tree-house shower offers the opportunity to bathe high in the verdant boughs and foliage of your favorite tree. This particular design is a magnet for children loving the adventurous opportunity of escaping skyward, much in the fashion of the characters of *The Swiss Family Robinson*. The tree-house shower can be a simple platform, or you can go to great lengths to create an entire treetop apartment featuring a bedroom, deck, and showering enclosure. Graywater can be collected in a tray beneath the shower platform and plumbed down to the ground, where it could empty into a dry well or be used to water the tree itself.

Reflect on Your Design

So, does your design include fanciful, freeform shapes or is it angular, clean, and meticulous in a different way? Are you drawn to curves or to straight lines and planes? Have you incorporated objects you could find in nature, such as tree trunks or boulders? Perhaps you know of an old, rusty wagon wheel that you passed while hiking one day that would make for an incredible design element? Do plants play a role in your mind's image of the shower — perhaps some gorgeous flowering vines attached to the main structure? Is your dream shower attached to a main building completely or partly, or is it entirely separate and on its own in a secluded glade or copse of trees?

Look carefully over your notepad. Are there any elements in your sketches that really speak to you? Are there parts, no matter how small or seemingly insignificant, that call back your eye again and again?

Keep looking over your drawings. Did you include a door? How does your door relate to the walls? Is it made from the same materials or something entirely different? If you used colors, what materials do the colors signify? Have you been storing in your garage for the past 10 years a box of terra-cotta tile that you purchased while vacationing in Mexico? Maybe those tiles were so extraordinary you just couldn't pass them up, so you haggled over a price with the shop owner and drove them home, and there they have lived ever since, waiting until this moment to be used. Suddenly, while you were madly sketching, you decided to use burnt sienna, and now you realize that those tiles are exactly that color and they were what you were thinking of all along.

The intricate wooden joinery and cedar grillwork of this shower requires more detailed planning than a simple minimalist backyard shower would.

Refine Your Design

Now the refinement begins. Choose the areas that stand out to you. Allow these details to guide your next drawings. This time start with the components you know you want to retain, and let the rest of the design evolve in relation to them. Maybe the areas that initially worked can be the starting point of a motif (a repeated design, shape, or pattern) that carries through the rest of the structure.

A preexisting building may already have a strong motif that you want to extend to the shower, or perhaps you want to create contrast and stylized tension with another aesthetic entirely. Either way, keep with the elements that work for you, and set aside the extraneous. You are panning for aesthetic gold, and eventually you will have a complete and perfect design.

By giving ample time and energy to this part of the design process, you will maximize your efficiency. It is far easier to redraw a design than it is to rebuild one. Save your precious resources of time, energy, and materials for building exactly what you want. But refine and re-refine your design until you are completely sure of what you want.

Your shower design will continue to mature and change as the construction process moves forward with each added material and visit to the building site. Your shower will not be fully complete until the plumbing solder has cooled, the mortar has dried between the stones, and the water is coursing down over your work-weary muscles.

The idea here is to retain enough intention and forward movement with the project that diligent work continues, while remaining open and flexible for new ideas and inspirations.

Create a Scaled Rendering

Once you have determined where you want your shower to be located, how it will be constructed, and what it will look like, you are ready to render (or draw to scale) the design (or share your ideas with a professional designer, who will create a scaled rendering for you). Drawing to scale means that you will draw an exact miniature of your structure in which a fraction of an inch on your drawing is equal to 1 foot at the actual shower site. Standard scaled drawings use ¼ inch and ½ inch to the foot. For example, if you are drawing a wall that is 8 feet high in ½-inch scale, the wall will be 4 inches high on paper. Or if a trellis is 6 feet wide, in ¼-inch scale it would be 1½ inches on paper. (In the metric system, scale drawings are prepared using ratios, such as 1:25 or 1:125, in whatever units the designer considers appropriate.)

You can use whatever increment is comfortable to work with, keeping in mind that the translation from foot to inch must be consistent and not too confusing to compute in your head (especially when dealing with fractions of the scale), and it must result in a scaled-down drawing that will fit on your paper.

The Stained Glass Nautilus Shower

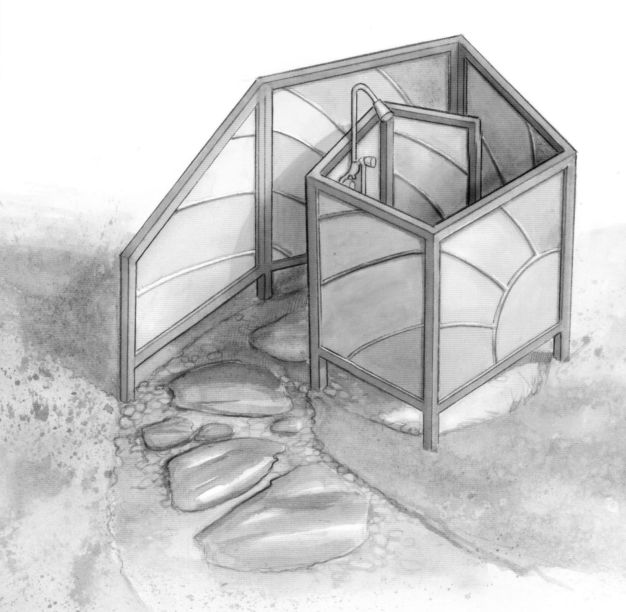

A shower created entirely out of stained glass will illuminate you with refracted, colored sunlight. Some people even believe that certain parts of the color spectrum affect your mood in different ways. Focus on an area of the spectrum you feel drawn to.

Graph paper helps considerably with this process because it is already laid out in a grid. You can purchase the few essential drafting tools from a local design, office, or art supply store. You will need the following: pencils, an eraser, graph or drafting paper, a drafting ruler (which is triangular and has scaled measurements along each edge), a plastic right-angle "square," any assortment of curved forms you may want to use, and a roll of tracing paper.

There are two basic ways to depict a structure in architectural drawing: the plan view, looking down on the structure from above, showing overall dimensions and the layout of the space, including relationships between different rooms and surrounding structures; and the elevation view, showing both the interior and the exterior of the structure, one wall or side at a time. Elevation drawings are very detailed in depicting all the architectural elements of the structure, including siding, trim, and hardware.

First, draw the plan view to scale, including the thickness of the walls, the direction in which the door will open, the benches, the towel rack, and so on, being sure to include all the fixed-in-place or built-in elements of your shower. Remember to include the overall length and width measurements of all such structures and fixtures.

Second, draw exterior views of each side of the shower, including the height and length measurements of all the special features you want to install, such as found objects, trellises, steps, windows, and wooden beams. Label each elevation drawing according to the directional side of the structure it shows (east, west, north, south), which will keep the orientation clear.

Once these drawings are complete, you can continue to refine your ideas by laying tracing paper over the scaled renderings and sketching out revisions on top. When you think that you have finally reached the point where you are satisfied with your drawings and there is no more to add, then make a final rendering of your drawings and let these be your working plans. Remember to keep all the sketches, scribbled drawings, and drafts of your plans filed in your construction journal for future reference.

The Ultimate Opportunistic Shower

Maui, Hawaii

ONE NEW YEAR'S MORNING, eight of us drove down a narrow and winding cliffside road on the remote Hana coast of Maui. Fifty feet below was a river that is often flooded by the heavy storms that pound the southern face of the 10,000-foot-high Haleakala Crater. These floods pour into steep ravines and create walls of water that devour trees, animals, and the occasional unsuspecting tourist.

On that day, we parked the trucks up the beach from the crushing surf break and walked single file into the enveloping jungle vegetation. Shafts of blazing sunlight and the sounds of distant and exotic mynah birds filtered down through the verdant gleam. We made our way hand over foot across river-slick boulders, being mindful of the treacherous algae-covered surfaces.

Soon I could make out the distant sound of a powerful torrent of water, and my pace quickened as I looked ahead to catch a glimpse of what I was hearing. In moments, a wave of mist hit me as I stared in disbelief at this paragon of nature — an 80-foot waterfall cascading down into a crystalline pool. With exaltations of glee, we plunged into the pool. I dove underwater and swam as far as one breath would carry me, emerging beneath the direct impact of this torrent of power.

The waterfall pounded my head and shoulders. All my strength was required to remain afloat and breathing while being stationed in the impact zone of this liquid free fall. It felt like marbles falling from the sky. I had never experienced this before; I wanted to move away, yet the moment felt all too precious.

Finally, I swam away and gazed at this incredible sight, a veritable Eden. Lush tropical vegetation grew enthusiastically on the surrounding cavernous walls. Among delighted friends cavorting and playing like children, I felt all was well on that New Year's morn.

Resources

ARCHITECTS

Blackbird Architects
Santa Barbara, California
805-957-1315
Venice, California
310-392-3150
www.bbird.com

Horst Buchanan Architects
Jamaica Plain, Massachusetts
617-524-6429
www.horstbuchanan.com

Lance Jay Brown Architecture and Urban Design
New York, New York
212-242-7966
lbrown147@aol.com

MacNelly Cohen Architects
West Tisbury, Massachusetts
508-693-4043
www.macnellycohen.com

LANDSCAPE ARCHITECTS

Jane MacLeish Landscapes
Washington, D.C.
202-966-8279
www.janes-garden.com

Stephen Stimson Associates
Falmouth, Massachusetts
508-548-8119
Boston, Massachusetts
617-578-8960
www.stephenstimson.com

DESIGNERS

Chance Anderson
Canterbury, New Hampshire
603-783-4490

Blackline Design Build
Oakland, California
510-663-8868
www.blacklinedb.com

Alexia Brue
Brooklyn, New York
212-929-5667
www.alexiabrue.com

Ethan Fierro
Kahului, Hawaii
808-872-1111
www.ethanfierro.com

Gary Harcourt
Against the Grain
Oak Bluffs, Massachusetts
508-693-7414

Jay Lagemann
Wild Island Sculpture
Chilmark, Massachusetts
jay@gowildisland.com
www.gowildisland.com

Steve Lohman
Line Art Gallery
West Tisbury, Massachusetts
508-693-4869
www.lineartgallery.com

SUPPLIERS

Gov Goleman
Metal Urges
Conway, Massachusetts
413-369-4451

T House
Ojai, California
805-646-7355
www.tonysthouse.com

MANUFACTURERS

Chicago Faucets
Des Plaines, Illinois
847-803-5000
www.chicagofaucets.com

Eljer
Dallas, Texas
800-423-5537
www.eljer.com

Halo Lighting
Cooper Industries
Peachtree City, Georgia
www.haloltg.com

Kohler
Kohler, Wisconsin
800-456-4537
www.kohler.com

Moen
North Olmsted, Ohio
800-289-6636
www.moen.com

OTHER READING

Cathedrals of the Flesh: My Search for the Perfect Bath. By Alexia Brue. Bloomsbury USA, 2003.

Bathrooms: Inspiring Ideas and Practical Solutions for Creating a Beautiful Bathroom. By Chris Casson Madden. Clarkson Potter, 1996.

Acknowledgments

It was the staff at Storey Publishing that first came up with the concept of a book on outdoor showers. I especially want to thank editorial director Deborah Balmuth, who guided the process through its early stages with such enthusiasm and support, as well as Dan Reynolds and Pam Art for their support and receptivity of this project.

I am grateful to my editor, Carleen Perkins, for her creativity, professionalism, and ebullience, considering the daunting task of sifting out the grain from the chaff of the original manuscript.

Also, a deep bow of appreciation for and acknowledgment that this book would not exist without the love and support of so many friends, family, and kindred spirits who agreed to let me include images of them and/or their showers and surroundings. They shared their knowledge and wisdom about aesthetics and technical challenges and emerged as a seamless web of interconnected voices, all sharing with this author his love of showering out of doors.

To the center of the "six degrees of separation" and dearest friend, Pamela Putney, who has provided sanctuary, creative guidance, encouragement, and tireless nurturing.

I specifically want to thank my mentor, Chance Anderson, wood and stoneworker extraordinaire, whose affectionate participation with the natural world has been a beacon and an inspiration.

And another bow to my woodworking sensei, Paul Tuller, who has lost sleep over finding creative solutions to my mechanical hurdles.

I want to also thank Michael Singer, friend and design genius, and my godfather, Dick Newick, whose world-class multi-hulls set the bar for excellence in physical manifestation when I was a teenager under his tutelage.

It was my mother Lee and my father Bernie who kinesthetically bore an adoration for the artistic approach to life and created the outdoor shower of my childhood, whetting my appetite for bathing outdoors.

And lastly, to my lifelong fellow adventurer and beloved wife, Phyllis, whose commitment, devotion, and boundless spirit has infused this entire process.

Under wet starlight
delicately massaging
rejuvenation

Index

Other Storey Titles You Will Enjoy

Be Your Own House Contractor, by Carl Heldmann.
The book to help you save 25 percent on building your own home
— without lifting a hammer!
176 pages. Paper. ISBN 978-1-58017-840-2.

Home Plan Doctor, by Larry W. Garnett.
The essential companion to buying home plans, from understanding
basic design principles to requesting needed modifications.
224 pages. Paper. ISBN 978-1-58017-698-9.

Hot Tubs, Saunas & Steam Baths, by Alan E. Sanderfoot.
A guide to planning your own home health spa — full-color photographs
show the range of designs available for both indoor or outdoor setting.
160 pages. Paper. ISBN 978-1-58017-549-4.

What Color Is Your Swimming Pool?, by Alan E. Sanderfoot.
Completely updated edition of this best-selling, easy-to-follow handbook
for caring for your pool.
208 pages. Paper. ISBN 978-1-58017-309-4.

Outdoor Stonework, by Alan and Gill Bridgewater.
A definitive guide to working with stone, from selecting and cutting stone
to preparing foundations and completing projects for your yard.
128 pages. Paper. ISBN 978-1-58017-333-9.

Rustic Retreats: A Build-It-Yourself Guide, by David and Jeanie Stiles.
Illustrated, step-by-step instructions for more than 20 low-cost, sturdy,
beautiful outdoor structures.
160 pages. Paper. ISBN 978-1-58017-035-2.

Stone Primer, by Charles McRaven.
The essential guide for homeowners who want to add the elegance
of stone, inside and out.
272 pages. Paper. ISBN 978-1-58017-670-5.
Hardcover with jacket. ISBN 978-1-58017-666-9.

These and other books from Storey Publishing are available
wherever quality books are sold or by calling 1-800-441-5700.
Visit us at _www.storey.com._